IMAGES
of America

ITALIAN-AMERICANS
IN RHODE ISLAND
VOLUME II

IMAGES
of America

ITALIAN-AMERICANS
IN RHODE ISLAND
VOLUME II

Joseph M. Muratore

ARCADIA
PUBLISHING

Published by Arcadia Publishing
Charleston SC, Chicago IL, Portsmouth NH, San Francisco CA

Printed in the United States of America

Library of Congress Catalog Card Number: 2006931586

For all general information contact Arcadia Publishing at:
Telephone 843-853-2070
Fax 843-853-0044
E-mail sales@arcadiapublishing.com
For customer service and orders:
Toll-Free 1-888-313-2665

Visit us on the Internet at www.arcadiapublishing.com

*I would like to dedicate this book to my family,
my wife, Rose, my son Joey, and my daughter Joy,
for the wonderful and full life they provided me with.*

COVER: THE EXTENDED FAMILIES OF FERRANTE, MAINELLI, LEONE, AND CRIBARI. This photograph was taken at a family reunion, in 1958, at the DiLorenzo's 1025 Club in Providence, Rhode Island. A few of the people pictured here, from left to right, are as follows: (front row) Emma Caliri, Pasquale Ferrante, Phyllis Cribari, Michael Mainelli, Etta Mainelli, Grace Gliottone, and Nicholas Leone; (second row) Micael Mainelli; (third row) Jean Ferrante; (fourth row) Joanne Moura, and Judith Burns; (fifth row) Shirley Winslow, Marietta Ferrante, Vera Ferrante, Lorna Mainelli, Regina Cribari, Rita Mainelli, and Marie Calvin; (sixth row) John Caliri, Marie Caliri, Nancy Caliri, Dr. Gaetano Ferrante, Josephine Ferrante, Joseph Cribari, and Dominic Mainelli; (back row) William Caliri, Donald Cribari, Paul Picozzi, Vincent DiChiara, William Feffant, and Nicholas Leone Jr.

CONTENTS

ACKNOWLEDGMENTS

In writing a book of this nature, it becomes necessary for the members of many families to give their time and knowledge in order to make each page more meaningful. I would like to thank the members of the many families that are included in this book, for their generosity in the time and information they have given. I would also like to thank the following: the members of the Coalition of Italian-American Organizations '76 Committee for their excellent work, during 1975–76, which I have drawn from; Mrs. Sandra Santomassimo, for her help in obtaining the strongest photos possible; and Mr. Robert Cribari, for furnishing photographs and material regarding the Ferrante and Cribari families. Lastly, I would like to to thank Mrs. Marjorie J. Gaule, my secretary, for the many hours she devoted in typing this manuscript onto a computer.

INTRODUCTION

It is amazing to realize the great number of immigrants that came from Italy to Rhode Island, especially during the period between 1890 and 1930. Their arrival was like floodgates being opened, and millions "poured forth" to America. These were immigrants who were leaving their hometowns becausethey could see no means of improving their standard of living, or of elevating their station in life. These immigrants were not only concerned for themselves, but for their children and families.

For most, finding a means of income was next to impossible, as they lived in suburbs where there were no factories or production plants, and, in many instances, no electricity, no municipal water system, few paved roads, and very basic educational systems. The convents, the churches, and the nuns, were the only initial source of education. If their parents were farmers, or if a parent had a skill such as being trained as a tailor, barber, or cook, the children, invariably, followed in the same type of work. The wages were so low that it was only enough to meet living expenses, and little, or nothing was left for savings.

To make matters worse, there was a monarchy governing, there was constant turmoil with wars, and nature was not kind. There were frequent earthquakes, volcanic eruptions, and uncontrollable floods.

These conditions did not prevail north of Rome, where work was more plentiful, which explains why so few immigrants from Northern Italy were early arrivals to America. Residents south of Rome were barely able to make a living, and each day was spent repeating the activities of the day before.

These immigrants were ready for a change. Soon after the Turco-Italian War was over in 1912, a large wave of over 32,000 immigrants came to Rhode Island. Following the World War I armistice, 32,493 more immigrants arrived in the area.

Between 1910 and 1930, the many immigrants that came to America were humble, hard-working people; they worked as farmers, laborers, and soldiers. They began to establish themselves and worked to support their families and to make their dreams come true.

There were over 100,000 Italian immigrants who came to Rhode Island during this period. It is interesting to think about what the early immigrants did to create income for themselves and their families. Some continued their trades or related jobs, "just to make a living." Others went into the jewelry, construction, and cutlery businesses. Those who entered the jewelry business, and the manufacturing of related products, provided jobs for such great numbers of people in

Rhode Island that, unknowingly, they played a significant role in the economic evolution that took place in Rhode Island.

The early significant manufacturers were the Uncas Manufacturing Company, the Imperial Knife Company (Felix Mirando), Trifari Jewelry, Carneglia, Vanerbec & Clois, the Calart California Artificial Flower Company, the Ronci Manufacturing Company, the Salvadore Tool Company, Tercat Tool & Die (Joseph Terino), Antonelli Plating, Campanella & Cardi, Ricci Enterprises, and McKendall Lumber. There were also many other employers who, collectively, created thousands of jobs.

These jobs were local and most people could walk to them, or take the electric trolley cars. As the trolley service was extended, more and more immigrants took jobs. It was these early job opportunities, created by the early arrivals, that attracted the immigrants to settle in Providence, which became one of the jewelry centers of the world.

These are but a few factors, that made the early arrivals hard workers, and, as families, ready to sacrifice and pool their resources. The results of their sacrifices are still evident today, in all walks of life in Rhode Island. I hope that this brief photographic chronology will help capture the recent past of the Italian Americans in Rhode Island, and show their tremendous progress in less than 100 years.

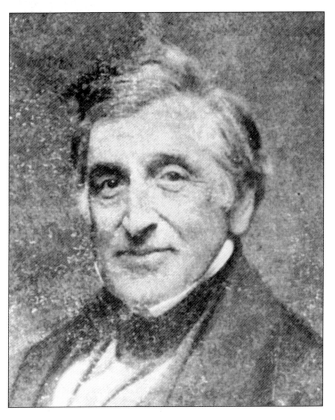

GIUSEPPE CARLO MAURANI (JOSEPH CARLO MAURANI M.D.). This immigrant was the first Italian to settle in Rhode Island, and the first Italian-American physician in Rhode Island. The son of Joseph Carlo Maurani, he was born in Barrington, R.I., on December 22, 1796. He was a graduate of Brown University, Class of 1816, and he attended Brown Medical School, where he received his M.D. degree, in 1819. Over the years, he spent much of his time between New York and Providence. He was consulting physician of Butler Hospital and Dexter Asylum, and was instrumental in the founding of Rhode Island Hospital. Giuseppe married Sophia Russell (Sterry) in 1820; he died in New York in 1873. (Courtesy of Gr "Uff" Joseph R. Muratore Collection.)

One

THE EARLY IMMIGRANTS AND THEIR FAMILIES

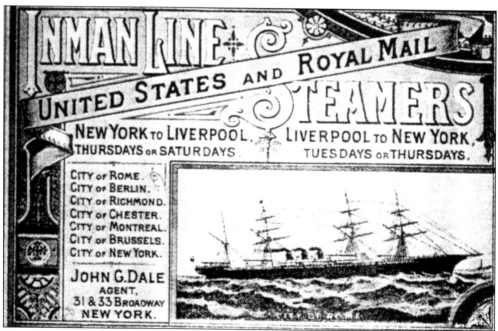

THE INMAN LINE SHIP ANNOUNCEMENT. In addition to the Fabre Line, which docked in Providence, many other ships carried thousands of Italian immigrants to the New England shores. Among the many ships was the *City of Rome*. Owned by the Inman Line, her maiden voyage was in October 1881. This was one of the poster announcements that listed its stops in Rome, Berlin, Richmond, Chester, Montreal, Brussels, and New York. (Courtesy of Gr "Uff" Joseph R. Muratore Collection.)

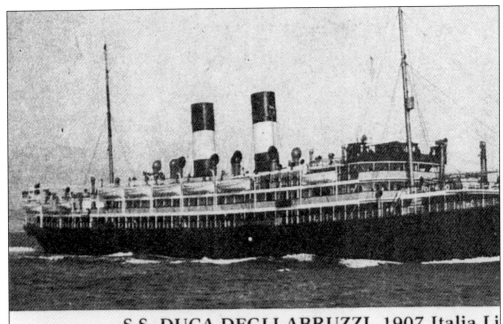

S.S. DUCA DEGLI ABRUZZI, 1907 Italia Li
Courtesy The Peabody Museum of Salem

SS *DUCA DEGLI ABRUZZI*, 1907 ITALIA LINE. This was one of the typical ships that brought thousands of early Italian immigrants to the American shores. The importance of these ships cannot be over emphasized. Each ocean crossing took between 21 and 29 days. It became an era that left a strong impression on the passengers; there were deaths, births, and romances that blossomed during the crossings. (Courtesy of The Peabody Museum of Salem.)

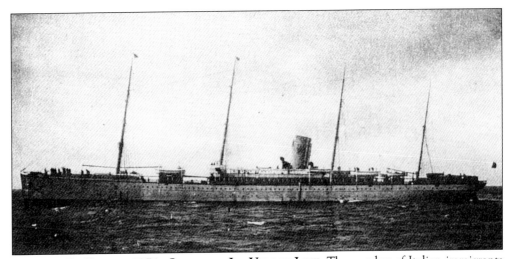

SS *CITTA DI NAPOLI*, 1871, OWNED BY LA VELOCE LINE. The number of Italian immigrants that made the crossing between 1870 and 1880 was 313. Between 1880 and 1890, 2,468; between 1890 to 1900, 8,972; between 1900 to 1910, 27,287; between 1910 and 1920, 32,241; and between 1920 and 1930, 32,493 crossed on the La Veloce Line. These were the years of the greatest wave of Italian arrivals to Rhode Island. (Courtesy of The Peabody Museum of Salem.)

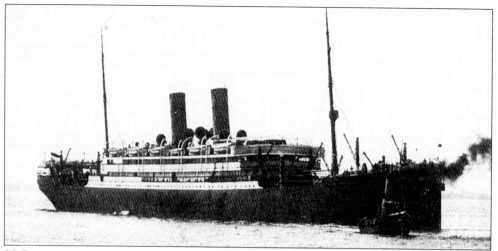

SS BARBAROSSA, 1896, OWNED BY THE NORTH GERMAN LLOYD LINE. It was on one of these ships that steerage-class passengers began to take on importance and that the "Patrone System" started. Mill owners and other manufacturers started to engage steamship ticket agents to act as employment agencies, who then recruited large numbers of Italians to bring to America. (Courtesy of The Peabody Museum of Salem.)

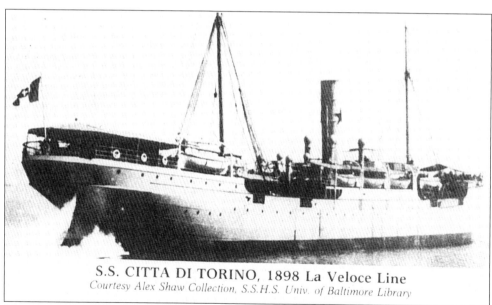

S.S. CITTA DI TORINO, 1898 La Veloce Line
Courtesy Alex Shaw Collection, S.S.H.S. Univ. of Baltimore Library

SS CITTA DI TORINO, 1898, OWNED BY THE LA VELOCE LINE. Due to the creation of the "Patrone System," the steamship agents began to build cold water flats and accommodate the early Italian arrivals. The agents financed the crossing tickets and the employment fees, and they provided funds for furniture, clothing, marriages, and burials. The system became an unwritten system of bondage. (Courtesy of Alex Shaw Collection, SSHS University of Baltimore Library.)

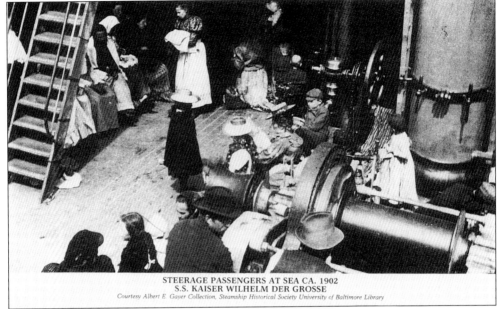

STEERAGE PASSENGERS AT SEA CA. 1902
S.S. KAISER WILHELM DER GROSSE
Courtesy Albert E. Gayer Collection, Steamship Historical Society University of Baltimore Library

PASSENGERS TRAVELING ABOARD THE SS *KAISER WILHELM DER GROSSE*, C. 1902. This type of ship was usually capable of carrying 550 first-class passengers and 800 passengers as steerage class. Other types of ship carried 220 first-class passengers and 900 third-class passengers. The price for first-class tickets ranged from $50 to $70 per person, while those traveling in steerage class paid only $26. Steerage passengers traveled together in the lower portion of the ship, where there were no dining halls or room separations. (Courtesy of Albert E. Gayer Collection, University of Baltimore Library.)

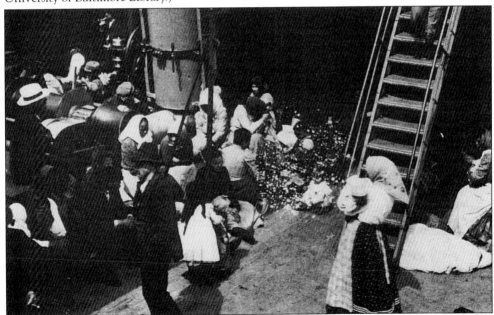

ABOARD THE SS *KAISER WILHELM DER GROSSE*, C. 1902. Steerage-class passengers were allowed one hour daily to go above board, in a designated section, so that they could enjoy the sunlight. (Courtesy of Albert E. Gayer Collection, University of Baltimore Library.)

Two

THE EARLY ARRIVALS

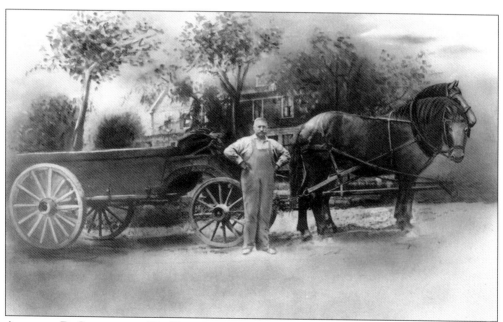

ANTONIO B. CARDI WITH HIS FIRST HORSE AND WAGON. Mr. Cardi started his construction company by digging cellars. Later, the Campagnella & Cardi Construction Company was formed, and it became one of the largest heavy construction companies in Rhode Island and Connecticut. The son of a merchant and a contractor, Mr. Cardi was born in 1873 in the town of Itri, five miles from the seaport of Gaeta. He married, in 1899, to Maria Civita Saccocio, and he came to the United States in 1900, arriving alone in New York, where he had to buy a hand shovel in order to obtain a job. For his first job, Mr. Cardi worked on the railroad from New York to Pennsylvania. He also worked the second shift, and was soon made a foreman. (Courtesy of Gr "Uff" Joseph R. Muratore Collection.)

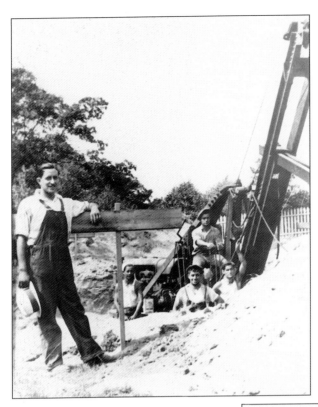

CARDI CONSTRUCTION COMPANY. Workmen are seen digging cellars. (Courtesy of Gr "Uff" Joseph R. Muratore Collection.)

AMERICO CARDI, BORN IN 1910. As a young man, Americo worked as a baker, washed cars, and delivered bread. In 1926, he left high school and went into business with his father. His father urged him to continue school but he did not return. In 1935, he married Jenette Maria Perrino of Cranston, and they became the parents of three children. In 1939, Americo merged the construction company with Campanella, and they began installing parking lots, as well as the pavement of the Scituate Reservoir. Cardi remained with Campanella for 29 years, and during this period they built many major highways, portions of Route 95, asphalt plants, and ready-mix plants in Rhode Island, Massachusetts, Connecticut, Virginia, New Jersey, and New York. In 1967, the partnership was divided and the Cardi Corporation was formed. (Courtesy of Gr "Uff" Joseph R. Muratore Collection.)

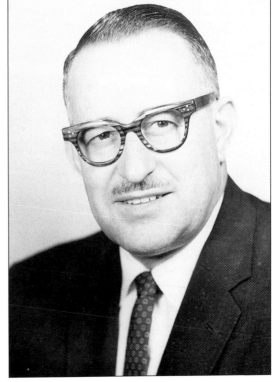

14

ANTONIO F. ROTELLI. Born in Minturno, Italy, in 1884, Antonio was one of six children. His father died when he was nine years old. At the age of 15, he left Italy and came to America, landing in 1901 in New York, where he had trouble finding employment. A month later Antonio came, on the Joy Line Steamer, to the Foxpoint section of Providence. He soon found employment as a water boy for a construction gang, and from that job, he joined a gang of 300 men who were building a railroad in Massachusetts. In a short time, he was promoted to foreman. Later, he went to work on the Branch Avenue sewer lines. When this job was completed, Antonio entered the construction business, building large commercial buildings in Rhode Island and New York City. Thereafter, he purchased land and buildings where the New England Ice Company was located, on Silver Lake Avenue. During that time, he also built two artificial ice(manufacturing plants in Boston. He built the first supermarket building in Cranston, and thereafter he continued to construct supermarket buildings. Antonio later became a wholesale liquor dealer in Providence. The business was operated by his grandsons, David, Michael, and Peter Aiello, until it was sold, in May of 1998, to a giant wholesale liquor distributor. In 1906, Antonio married Assunta D'Ascoli, and they became the parents of four sons and two daughters. (Courtesy of Gr "Uff" Joseph R. Muratore Collection.)

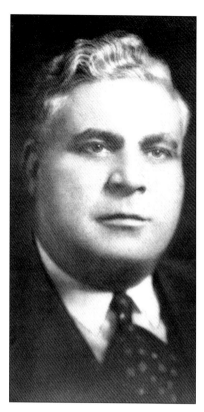

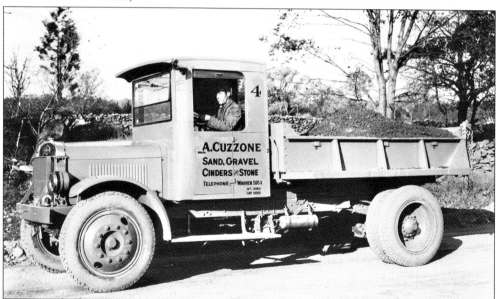

ANTONIO CUZZONE. This man was the first Italian to be employed at Nayatt Brick Yard, in 1895. He was the father of Angelo Cuzzone, who, in 1912, established the first Italo-American sand and gravel business in Barrington, where he operated it until 1945. (Courtesy of Gr "Uff" Joseph R. Muratore Collection.)

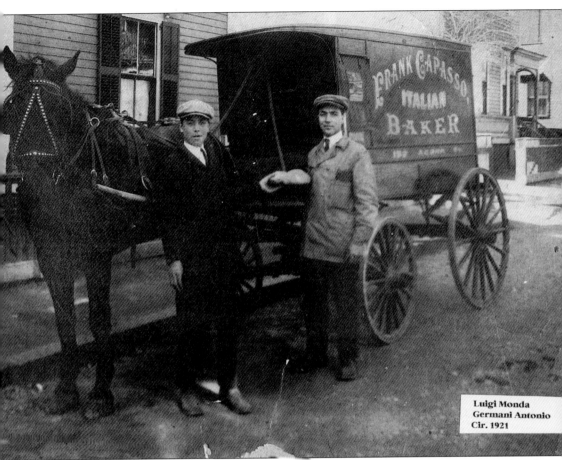

Luigi Monda
Germani Antonio
Cir. 1921

LUIGI MONDA, "THE KING OF BREAD." Luigi developed one of the first home-delivery bread routes in Rhode Island and he became known as "The King of Bread" on Federal Hill. He was born in Naples, Italy, to Giachino and Jennie Monda. Having received no formal education, Luigi came alone, in 1912, to America, where he found employment in a macaroni factory in Cleveland, Ohio. Shortly thereafter he came to Providence, where his first job was with Nicholson File Company on Acorn Street. He was unhappy with an indoor job, so when he became friendly with John Del Sesto, who was working for Capasso's Bakery on Acorn Street, they developed a small route for Luigi, with a horse and wagon, delivering Capasso's bread. John Del Sesto, who later owned an excellent pastry shop, guided Luigi Mondo to earn the reputation of "The King of Bread." In 1915, Luigi married Rosina Fiore at the Holy Ghost Church, and they became the parents of four children. Bread, at that time, sold for 3, 6, and 9 cents per loaf, and with the Depression prevailing, many of his customers could not afford to pay. However, Luigi continued to deliver bread, and many times he would wipe the customer's name off his records, marking it paid. Luigi Monda died on January 5, 1974. Pictured in the photograph are Luigi Mondo and Tony Germani, c. 1916. (Courtesy of Gr "Uff" Joseph R. Muratore Collection.)

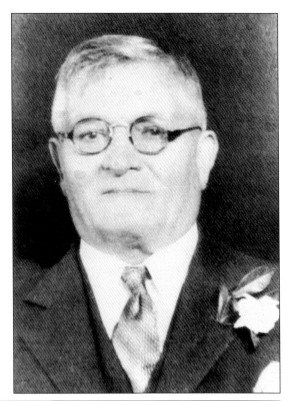

GILICERO PERRINO, FOUNDER OF CRANSTON FARMS, INC. Gilicero was born in Gallo, province of Compobasso, Italy, the son of Michele and Angelina (Paulo) Perrino. In 1892 he came to America. He settled in Providence, R.I., and in 1901 he started his own dairy business with one cow on Federal Hill. He married Rosa Boiano, and they had four children: Michael, Anthony, John, and Anna. His entire family worked at the dairy business until it closed and the land on Park Avenue was sold. (Courtesy of Gr "Uff" Joseph R. Muratore Collection.)

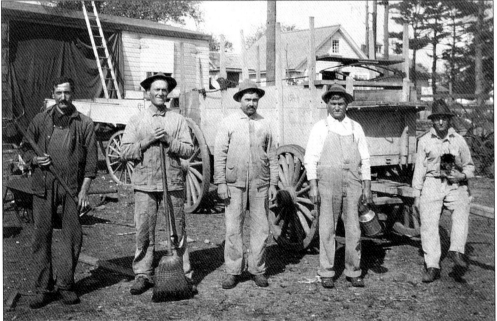

CRANSTON DAIRY FARM WORKERS. Among the workers pictured here are farmhand Antonio Perrino, a cousin of the family; a cousin of grandfather Gilicero; and Michael Perrino, the oldest son. The photograph was taken at the Cranston Farm location, c. 1935. (Courtesy of Gr "Uff" Joseph R. Muratore Collection.)

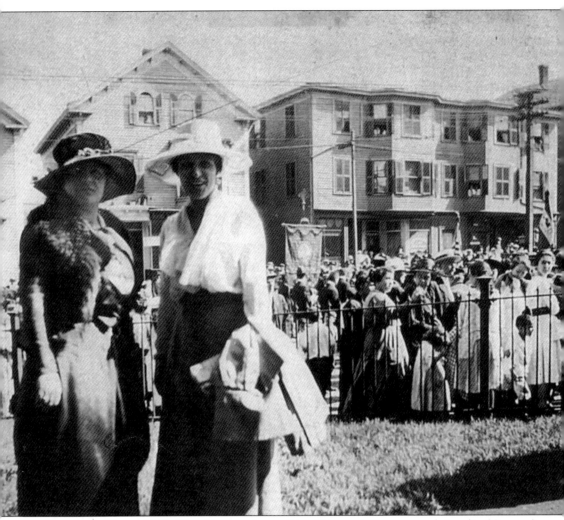

COLUMBUS DAY, 1918. The Capone sisters, Liza (Capone) Gattone and Amalia (Capone) Pettine, are pictured, watching the parade and waiting for the speaker's program to begin, in front of the Atwells Avenue schoolyard. Across the street can be seen the building, at 248 Atwells Avenue, of the A.E. Ventrone Wholesale Grocery Store, where the Macaroni Riot took place in 1914. (Courtesy of Gr "Uff" Joseph R. Muratore Collection.)

PETER MELARAGNO, ONE OF THE PIONEER BUSINESSMEN ON FEDERAL HILL. With his piano music roll, cigar, and newspaper store, Mr. Melaragno created a true emporium. Many people would visit him at the 299 Atwells Avenue store, where cigars were made. A wide variety of goods, from newspapers to opera scores, were sold here. Every day, Mr. Melaragno would hang the most popular newspapers from inside his store window, so that the public could read the headlines. (Courtesy of Gr "Uff" Joseph R. Muratore Collection.)

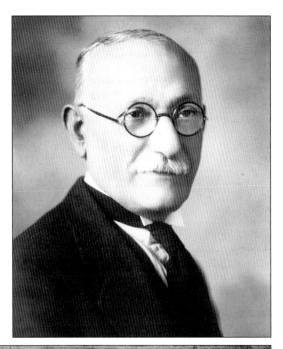

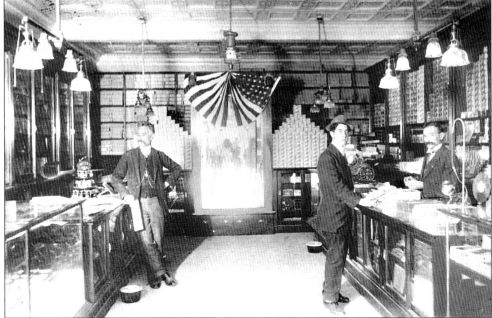

PETER MELARAGNO IN HIS STORE. This was the scene where, during the Macaroni Riot, Mr. Melaragno allowed many men to come into his store when the police were in pursuit of them. He had so many men in his store that they stood on counters and behind the store, and when the police came to make arrests, Mr. Melaragno would not allow them to enter. He asked that they produce warrants, and when they did not have the correct documents, he did not allow them to enter. By his actions, he prevented many of the local innocent bystanders from being arrested. Mr. Melaragno is pictured to the far right of the photograph, c. 1916. (Courtesy of Gr "Uff" Joseph R. Muratore Collection.)

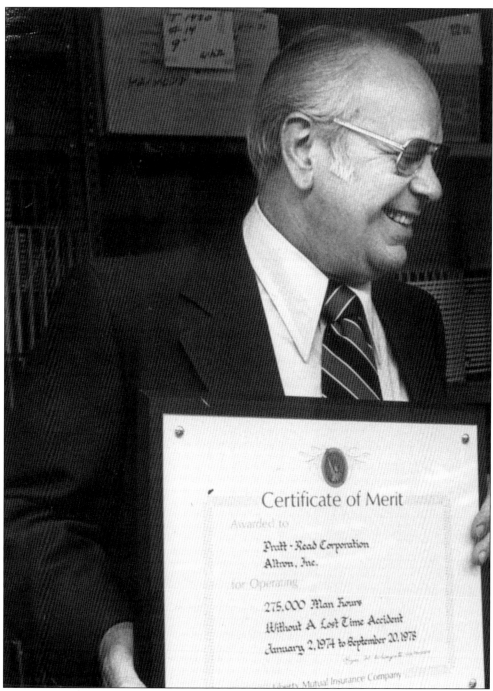

MANRICO R. MELARAGNO, SON OF PETER MELARAGNO. Manrico is shown receiving the Certificate of Merit Award, October 1982, in recognition for 27 years of service as founder and president of Altron Inc. of Westerly, Rhode Island. The company, which produced a variety of electric coils and electro-mechanical devices, was acquired by Pratt-Read in 1964. Manrico received his Bachelor of Science degree in electrical engineering at the University of Rhode Island. (Courtesy of Gr "Uff" Joseph R. Muratore Collection.)

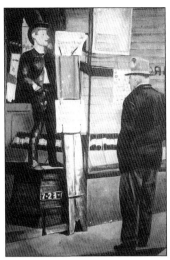 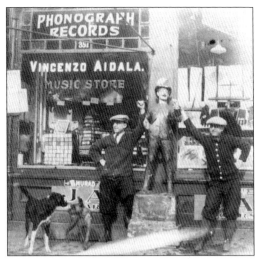

LEFT: THE AIDALA NEWSPAPER AND PIANO MUSIC ROLL STORE. This store was located at 351 Atwells Avenue in Providence, and operated by Mr. Vincenzo Aidala. This was a favorite meeting place, where men would read the newspaper headlines and have all-day discussions, regarding what was going on in Rhode Island and in their hometowns. In front of the store stood a majestic-looking mannequin of an English racetrack starter, which became a favorite landmark for people to decide where they would meet. The mannequin became a landmark around 1910. (Courtesy of Gr "Uff" Joseph R. Muratore Collection.) RIGHT: THE AIDALA PIANO MUSIC ROLL, CIGAR, AND NEWSPAPER STORE. Pictured at this meeting place are, from left to right, Joseph Aidala, and Tom Aidala, c. 1910. (Courtesy of Gr "Uff" Joseph R. Muratore Collection.)

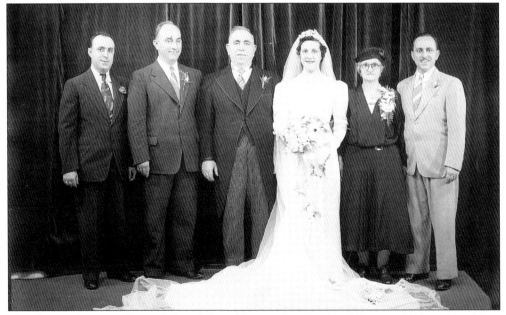

THE AIDALA FAMILY. Pictured, from left to right, are, Joseph, Tom, Vincenzo (father,) Josephine, Lucia (mother,) and Frank. Vincenzo and Lucia, as well as their children, from time to time, all worked in the store as a family unit. Lucia was an excellent Italian cigar maker. (Courtesy of Gr "Uff" Joseph R. Muratore Collection.)

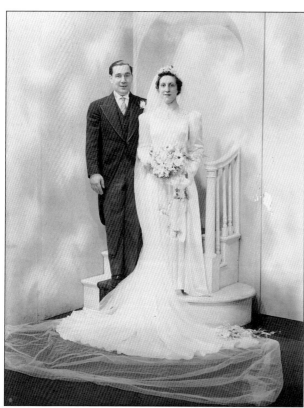

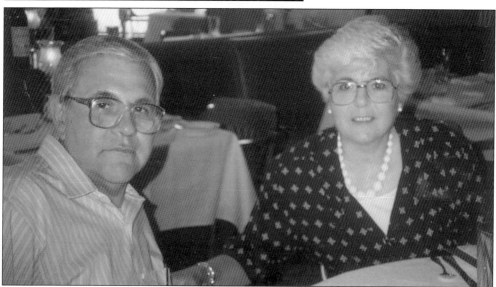

FRANK AND JEAN (LILLIAN MANOOGIAN) D'ANTUONO. After the closing of their music store, Frank and Jean opened a grocery store, which carried a complete line of Italian groceries. In 1981, they closed the store, remodeled the building and opened an Italian Trattoria, serving excellent food. It became a popular meeting place, not only for the local residents, but also for people from everywhere, including those who were returning to Federal Hill to visit. (Courtesy of Gr "Uff" Joseph R. Muratore Collection.)

"Don" Raffaele De Angelis and His Wife, Virginia (Del Rossi) De Angelis. Virginia was the daughter of Gaetano Del Rozzi, one of the largest macaroni manufacturers at that time. Don Raffaele, a registered pharmacist, was born in Teano, Italy, in 1878. He attended public schools in his hometown and at eight years old he began to work in a pharmacy. In 1904, he came to Providence. His main assets were his knowledge of pharmacy, his ambition to work, and to become successful. Soon after he established himself in Rhode Island, he began to manufacture citrate of magnesia, a product that bore his name as a trademark. In a short time, his business grew so rapidly that he erected a building at 131 Knight Street, where he began to manufacture pharmaceutical products. He employed seven registered pharmacists in his drug store, which filled prescriptions only. Everyone called him "Don" as a title of respect, and if anyone who could not pay for medicine, he would say "pay me later." Many of those who could not afford payment would bring him eggs and homegrown vegetables, although Don was known to discourage this practice. (Courtesy of Gr "Uff" Joseph R. Muratore Collection.)

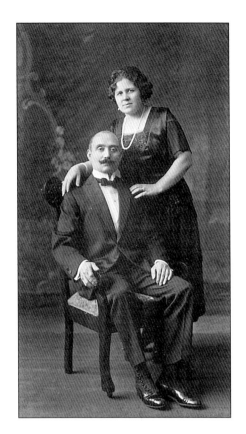

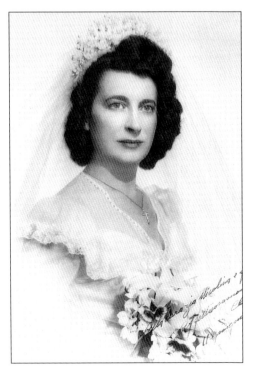

Clorina (Amicarelli) DeAngelis, the Daughter of Almerinda (Melaragno) and Antonio Amicarelli. After his first wife died in 1945, "Don" Raffaele De Angelis married Clorina (Amicarelli) DeAngelis, a member of the distinguished Melaragno family. She, and 10 other children, left Italy to make a new life for themselves in the New World. Some came to America, some went to Buenos Aires, and some came to Rhode Island. Imagine the pain and anguish that the parents suffered when 11 of their children gradually left the family home and came to make a new life in the New World. Parents knew that once their children left, they would perhaps never see or hear their voices again, as there were no telephones, no air travel, no fax machines, and travel was only by ship, taking from 21 to 29 days to make the crossing. In many instances, once children left, the only communication their parents would have was by writing letters, which would take 30 days or more to be delivered. (Courtesy of Gr "Uff" Joseph R. Muratore Collection.)

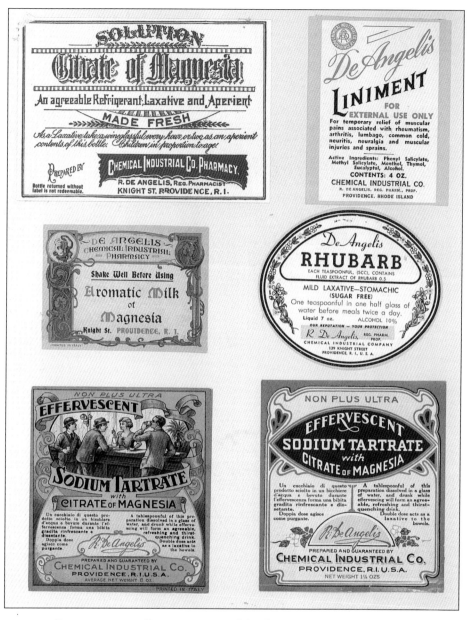

SOME OF THE LABELS FOR THE PRODUCTS THAT MR. DEANGELIS MANUFACTURED. The wide variety of pharmaceutical products manufactured was truly amazing. Mr. DeAngelis was the pioneer of many products that can still be seen on drug-store shelves today. The labels, which he designed, were black, gold and vivid red, and many of them were made in Italy and applied to his products in America. The author, who was privileged to have known "Don" Raffaele, was requested after his death to preserve as much of the machinery, equipment, and labels as possible. An attempt to donate these items to local societies and museums was unsuccessful because the collection was so vast that none of the local organizations would undertake the task of preserving and cataloging them. The building where this pharmacy was operated is still in existence today. (Courtesy of Gr "Uff" Joseph R. Muratore Collection.)

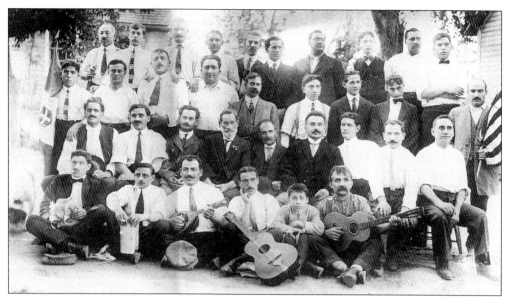

THE ISERNIA CLUB. The members of this club were from Isernia, Italy. This club was typical of many others that were formed as a means for those from particular towns to make friends with people who could speak their native language. Often, these members had common interests, such as being musical, and they developed Bocce clubs and other gathering places, where early settlers would go to exchange ideas and help one another to find jobs and establish themselves. In the center of this photograph is Giuseppe Pettine, c. 1915. (Courtesy of Gr. "Uff" Joseph R. Muratore Collection.)

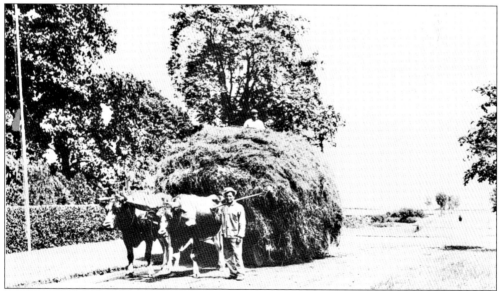

AN EARLY BARRINGTON SETTLER, LEADING AN OXEN-DRAWN CART UP PRIMROSE HILL. This land, which was part of the Odamquin Farm, was purchased by the Peck family from the Sowams tribe in 1653. Barrington was a large farming community in the early 1900s, and it attracted many Italian immigrants who had farming skills. They cultivated the land, and made a living for themselves and their families. (Courtesy of Gr "Uff" Joseph R. Muratore Collection.)

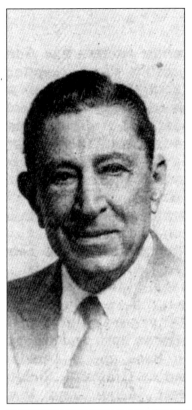

PETER J. CALADRONE. Peter was born on Federal Hill on September 2, 1886, the son of Nicola and Carmina (Conca) Caladrone. Educated in the local public schools, he graduated LaSalle Academy. He worked with his father, who opened one of the first banking and steamship offices at 39 Spruce Street, Providence, in 1896. In 1919, when Peter was 33 years old, he constructed a building at 295 Atwells Avenue and started his own business. He first went into the insurance business, but then opened a travel agency, and became a pioneer travel agent in Rhode Island. He founded the Inter State Motor Coach Company, which operated coaches between Providence, North Scituate, Worcester, Attleboro, and other local routes. In 1911, Peter was elected to the General Assembly, and in 1918, he was elected councilman for the 9th ward, serving until 1924. He was director of the Morris Plan Bank and Plantations Bank for 40 years. He was also director of the Cycledrone, which owned the Providence Steam Rollers Football Team. It was Peter's determination that resulted in the building of Kenyon Street School, and the widening of Atwells Avenue. He married Rose Josephine (Cappelli) on April 6, 1915. They became the parents of Nicholas J. and William E., two sons. Peter had three brothers, Angelo A., Albert A., and Dr. Charles V., and a sister, Mrs. Elizabeth DiChiara. (Courtesy of Gr "Uff" Joseph R. Muratore Collection.)

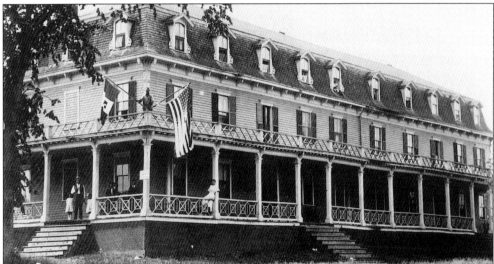

THE LONGMEADOW HOTEL AND CASINO, LOCATED IN THE LONGMEADOW, RIVER VUE SECTION OF WARWICK. It was within walking distance of the Narragansett Bay. Many early arrivals would rent two rooms for a week, so that they and their families could enjoy the benefits of the sun and sea. This became a very popular location and it was often booked a year ahead. The author later sold this building in the mid-1960s. The new owners carefully disassembled the building, from which the lumber and material was sufficient to build three homes. (Courtesy of Gr "Uff" Joseph R. Muratore Collection.)

Federal Hill Community Organizations in the Neighborhood, 1915–1919

Acorn
146   Rossaria MS Society
America
    America Street Public School
62   First Italian Methodist Church
100½   Italo-American Club
Arthur
36   Isola D'Ischia Club
68   Frosolonese Club
74   Teanese Club
    La Galazzia Club
88   Toscano Club
    Federal A. Club
109   E. De Amicis Socialist Club
111   Sons of Italy Club
Atwells
    Franklin Park Bath House
120   Italo-American Club
142   Garibaldi Club
173   L'Eco Del Rhode Island
189½   Sergniese Social Club
200r   Liberty and Prosperity Political Club
206   Carlo Marx Club
207   Workingmen's Independent Political Club
    T. Salvini CD Club
    Rossini Club
209   Italo-American Progressive Club
    Atwells Avenue Primary School
213½   Young Federal A Club
221   Ninth Ward Independent Political Club

238   Verdi Club
296   Fratone Italiane
    Italian Literary and Political Club
298   Italian City Public Works Employees Club
    La Basilicata Club
300   Isernia Social Club
    Ninth Ward Protective Club
331   Pietra Vairano Club
393   Atwells Athletic Club
397   Donefro Club
    Filodramatical Club
399   Dante Alighieri Club
400   Federal Hill House
433   Circolo Cittadini Italian del 14 Dist.
472   Holy Ghost Church
Dean
71   Frosolonese Club
139   Federal Hill Baptist Church
140   Young Federal A Club
151   L'Eco Del RI Printing
Federal
    Federal Street Grammar School
    Federal Street Primary School and Kindergarten
146   Il Corriere Del Rhode Island
Knight
40   Royal Band
    Knight Street School
Spruce
    Benevolence Hall

LISTING OF ITALIAN-AMERICAN SOCIAL AND POLITICAL ORGANIZATIONS. These organizations were in existence between 1915 and 1920 in Providence. It is interesting to note how quickly the various groups were formed, and the locations of the clubs and meeting places. Some of the interesting and unusual clubs, listed here, are the Garibaldi Club, the Liberty and Prosperity Political Club, the Carlo Marx Club, and the Workingmen's Independent Political Club. There was a good cross-section of various interests, and the clubs provided a meeting place for those with similar interests to meet and talk in their native language. (Courtesy of Gr "Uff" Joseph R. Muratore Collection.)

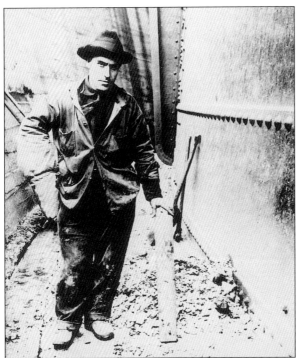

THE PROVIDENCE GAS COMPANY. The new immigrants were without knowledge of the American language, and many, with families to support, had little to offer but their strength and their willingness to support themselves and their families. The Providence Gas Company was at the forefront of employing immigrant labor, and it was these immigrants' hard labor and willingness to work that helped build the Providence Gas Company .In turn, the growth of this organization aided the rapid development of the city of Providence. These same immigrants had heard in Italy that "there was gold in the streets of America," but no one told them that they had to dig and lay the streets before they could get the "gold." (Courtesy of Gr "Uff" Joseph R. Muratore Collection.)

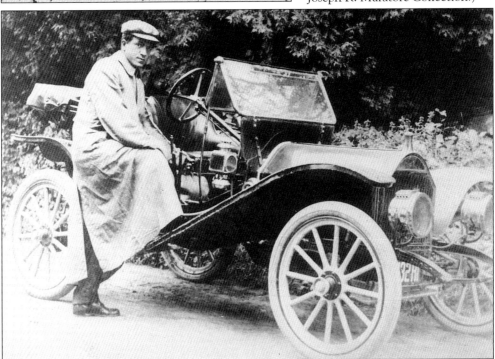

THE CAR AND MAN. This was a two-seater, which was a very popular type of car around 1910. For anyone that was able to buy one of these cars, it was a sign that they had made it and that they were able to afford some of the luxuries that this great country had to offer. (Courtesy of Gr "Uff" Joseph R. Muratore Collection.)

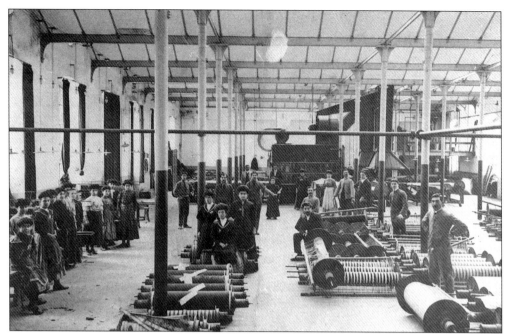

EARLY IMMIGRANTS IN THE WANNASQATUCKET TEXTILE MILLS. These immigrants were willing to learn a trade; and they were also ambitious and motivated. Employers quickly noticed the advantages of employing such people, not only for their ability, but also for their willingness to work at hard jobs for long hours. (Courtesy of Gr "Uff" Joseph R. Muratore Collection.)

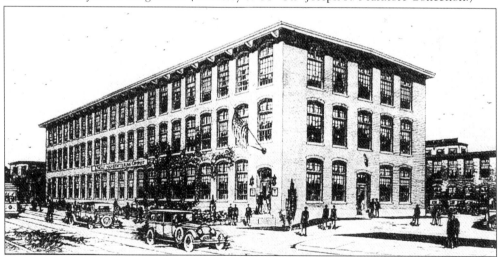

THE UNCAS MANUFACTURING COMPANY, FOUNDED BY CAV. VINCENT SORRENTINO IN 1911. Located at 623–631 Atwells Avenue, Providence, it became the world's largest ring-manufacturing plant, creating 800 jobs for immigrants. Vincent Sorrentino came to America in 1906 from Castellamare di Stabia, Naples, and in a few years, established the plant, which was originally located at 9 Calendar Street. The company was later moved to Sprague Street, and then again, in 1929, to a larger building at 623–631 Atwells Avenue. In 1911, he married Katie Goldstein. They became the parents of seven children, Anna Marie, Loretta Louisa, Helena Evelyn, Dorothy Edna, Louis Vincent, Gloria Virginia, and Stanley Lawrence. (Courtesy of Gr "Uff" Joseph R. Muratore Collection.)

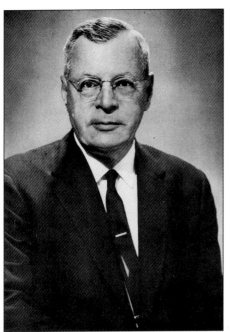

DR. FELIX A. MIRANDO. Dr. Mirando was born in Frosolone, in the province of Campobasso, Italy. He came to America at an early age, and settled in Providence. With his brother, Michael, and a friend, Domenic Fazzano, he cofounded the Imperial Knife Company in 1916, enabling the three men to put into practice the skills they had learned in their native land. Dr. Mirando later became president of the Imperial Knife Company. He was a director of Industrial National Bank, Old Colony Cooperative Bank, Narragansett Electric Company, Providence Washington Insurance Company, and the New England Electric System, as well as many other charitable service organizations. He was a recipient of numerous citations, awards, and honorary degrees. He married Aurora (DiNoce) and they became the parents of four children. (Courtesy of Gr "Uff" Joseph R. Muratore Collection.)

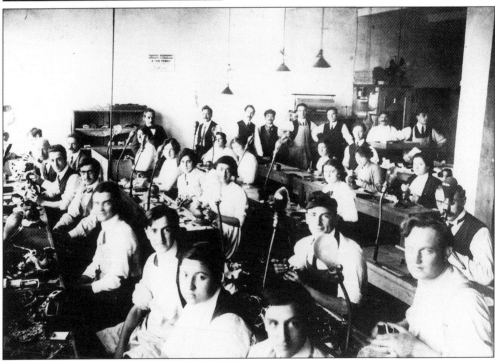

TRIFARI JEWELRY WORKERS AT THEIR BENCHES. This was a typical production-line work area at the Trifari Jewelry Company, which provided more than 500 jobs for early Italian immigrants in Rhode Island. Trifari, Krishna and Fishel Inc. established a new plant at 3400 Pawtucket Avenue, East Providence, and Gustavo Trifari Jr. became the executive vice-president. The organization became one of the largest jewelry manufacturers in the world. (Courtesy of Gr "Uff" Joseph R. Muratore Collection.)

VITO CARNEGLIA. Vito, born in Ischia, began his employment with the Uncas Manufacturing Company and, within 10 years, he became its vice president. He later co-purchased, with others, the Clark and Cooms Co., the oldest ring company in the United States, and for 40 years he served as its president. He was a prominent Catholic layman, and a major benefactor of Providence College. He married Theresa, and they became the parents of two children, Doris and Donald. (Courtesy of Gr "Uff" Joseph R. Muratore Collection.)

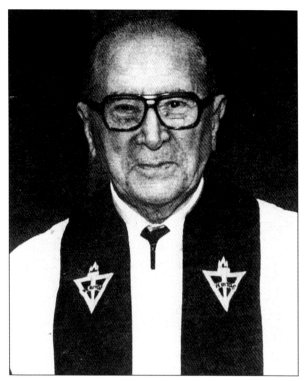

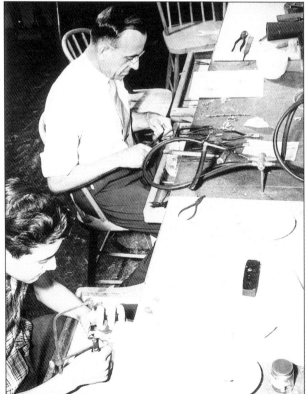

SKILLED JEWELRY WORKERS MAKING JEWELRY SAMPLES. This scene shows the workers in one of the early jewelry shops. Many of the early Italian immigrants that were given the right opportunity, developed into skilled pattern makers, model makers, and mold makers. (Courtesy of Gr "Uff" Joseph R. Muratore Collection.)

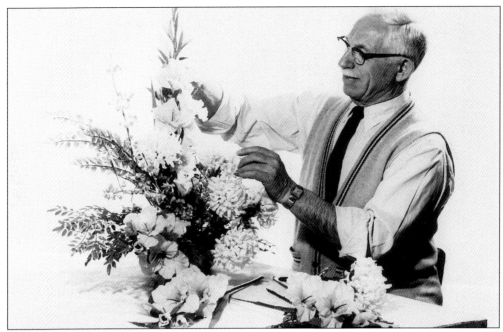

MICHELE D'AGNILLO, ADDING MASTERFUL FINISHING TOUCHES TO HIS FLORAL ARRANGEMENT DESIGN. Michele was born in Agnone, in the province of Compobasso, Italy, on April 6, 1894. He was the son of Donato Nicolo and Antonietta (Pannunzio) D'Agnillo. At 17 years old, he immigrated to America, where he worked in foundries, copper mines, vineyards, and orchards. In 1920, he returned to Italy, and married Giuseppina Iacabone in 1921. Michele then returned to America and settled in Providence, and in 1922, his wife joined him. They were the parents of one son. His hobby of making flowers developed into a life long means of livelihood. With the help of his wife, he made flowers that Cherry & Webb Company bought. His first order was for $5, and the Outlet Company bought his second order for $200. His business, Calart Company, was started in a tenement house on Spruce Street. When the business grew, he moved to 32 Broadway, and then later again to Westminster and Snow Streets. His flowers were distributed throughout America, Mexico, Canada, and England. In 1939, Michele built a factory and office building at 400 Reservoir Avenue, Providence, where he employed more than 700 people. (Courtesy of Gr "Uff" Joseph R. Muratore Collection.)

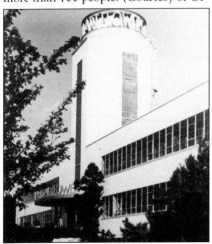

CALART COMPANY BUILDING. This location, at 400 Reservoir Avenue, was where the beautiful artificial floral arrangements, and all other Calart creations, were made and assembled. Later, component parts of flowers were made in Hong Kong and assembled in Providence. This building was constructed in 1939. Today it is surrounded by 7 acres of landscaped grounds, surrounded by an abundance of trees and flowers of every kind. The grounds are park-like in appearance, and many wedding pictures have been taken here. (Courtesy of Gr "Uff" Joseph R. Muratore Collection.)

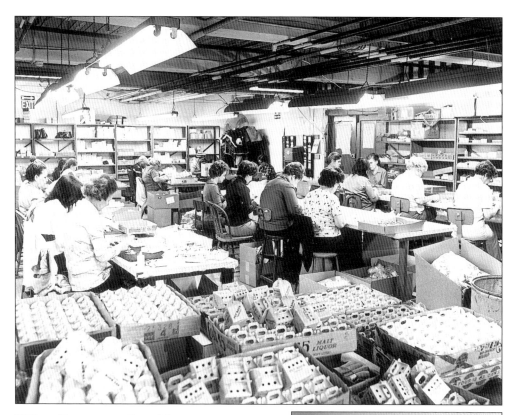

D'Orio Enterprises Inc., Manufacturers of Jewelry and Novelty Jewelry Products. During the 1970s and 1980s, this business experienced phenomenal growth, which required a plant expansion and the employment of 500 people to work on the company's contracts. This is a view of one of D'Orio's assembly rooms. (Courtesy of Gr "Uff" Joseph R. Muratore Collection.)

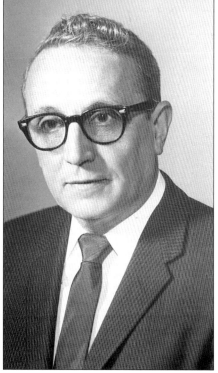

Angelo Del Sesto, Founder, President, and Treasurer of Van Dell Corp. Angelo was an accomplished and talented jewelry designer, and he served as instructor of jewelry design at Rhode Island School of Design for 19 years. His famous jewelry creations were designed using cultured pearls with delicate leaves and scrolls of gold in pin form, and bracelets in a geometric design. He was a director of Columbus National Bank, Jewelers Board of Trade, and many other corporations. He was also an active member of many charitable Italian-American organizations. Angelo was born in Providence on June 10, 1896, the son of Antonio and Maria (Tella) Del Sesto. In 1930, he married Sarah (Devlin). (Courtesy of Gr "Uff" Joseph R. Muratore Collection.)

33

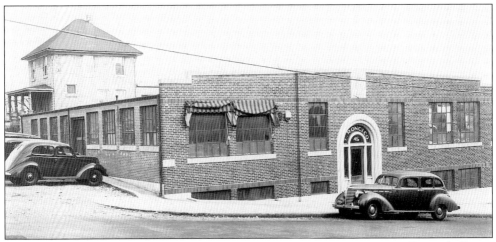

RONCI MANUFACTURING COMPANY AT 45 RIVER AVENUE, PROVIDENCE. Fernando Ronci established this company in 1918, when he was 25 years old. Later, in 1927, he moved the business to the River Avenue location. Fernando was born in Carve, in the province of Rome, Italy. He was the son of Franceso and Nazzarena (Donnini) Ronci, with whom he came to America in 1910. (Courtesy of Gr "Uff" Joseph R. Muratore Collection.)

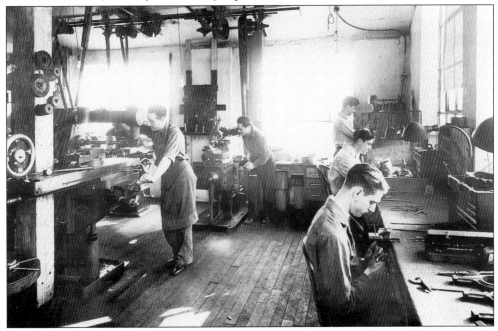

GENERAL VIEW OF THE RONCI MANUFACTURING COMPANY. This photograph was taken c. 1936, during the early years of development, as is apparent by the overhead leather pulley-belts that were used to work the machinery. Later, when motors became more available, the equipment was modernized and more fully mechanized. Here, skilled workers perform many of the operations for the diverse lines of jewelry and other products. Romco companies became the parent company for Ronci Manufacturing. It employed more than 550 people throughout Rhode Island and the United States. Ronci Manufacturing was an employment center that many early settles and their families worked at. (Courtesy of Gr "Uff" Joseph R. Muratore Collection.)

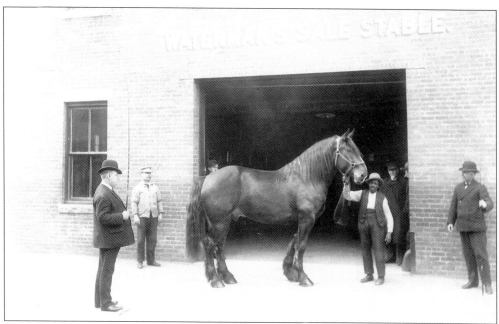

SALVADORE TOOL & FINDINGS INC. This company was founded in the cellar of Andrea Salvadore's home, at 1446 Chalkstone Avenue, in 1945. Shortly thereafter, his brother Ameleto joined him. When another brother, Joseph, joined them in 1946, they moved to 71 Troy Street in the Oneyville section of Providence. In 1952, they moved from Troy Street to their present location, 369 West Fountain Street, the former Waterman Stable Sales Company, which has undergone extensive renovations and architectural improvement additions. The brothers' parents were Michele and Maria Garcia (Constantino) Salvadore, who were born in Santa Polinare, in the province of Frosolone, Italy. They were the parents of eight children. Andrea, Ameleto and Joseph were born in America. The business, which engages in the designing and production of jewelry tools and jewelry findings, is operated today by Ameleto, his two sons, Stephen and Thomas, and daughter, Claire, as well as Joseph's children, David and Christopher.

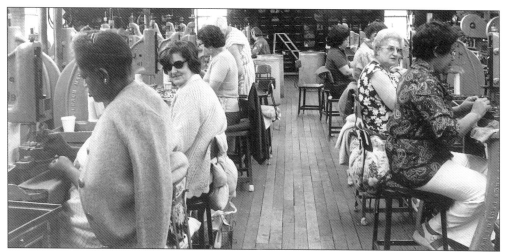

FOOT PRESS OPERATORS' ROOM. This room was at the Salvadore Tool & Findings Company, which employed 105 people. (Courtesy of Gr 'Uff' Joseph R. Muratore Collection.)

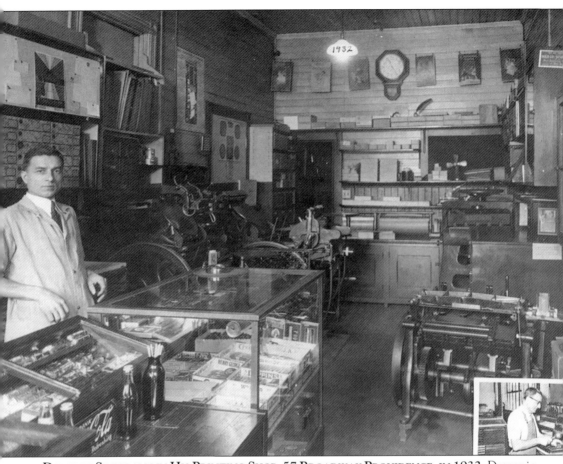

DOMENIC SINISGALLI IN HIS PRINTING SHOP, 57 BROADWAY PROVIDENCE, IN 1932. Domenic was born in Boston, Massachusetts, in 1893. His parents returned to Italy with him in 1896, and they remained in Italy until he was 10 years old. As a young man, Domenic sold newspapers and helped his father at their fruit store. He attended schools in Somerset, Massachusetts. At 13 years old, he went with his grandmother and uncle, Frank Solitto, to work at his uncle's shoe shine stand and grocery store. In this way, they earned a living, and were able to send small amounts of money to their family in Italy. Domenic closed the shoe shine shop and went to work for the Franklin Press, before coming to Providence, where he went to work at the *Providence Journal* as a typesetter. He also returned to school and earned his high school diploma. In 1916, he married Rosalie (Borecca). They became the parents of two daughters, Dorothy (Sinisgalli) Testa, and Marianne (Sinisgalli) Lombardi. In 1921, he established the Quality Press at 62 Federal Street, Providence. In 1923, the shop was moved to 57 Broadway. In 1926, Domenic purchased his first automated printing press. During the next 34 years, numerous governors and Rhode Island notables commissioned him for their design and printing needs. In 1960, he sold the printing company, and the shop was later acquired by Mercury Mail Advertising Inc. of Pawtucket. It is at this location that the original Miller press and memorabilia exists today, as it was in 1920. Domenic died in 1978. (Courtesy of Gr "Uff' Joseph R. Muratore Collection.)

JOSEPH TERINO. Joseph was born in 1916 in Providence. In 1936, at the age of 20, he established Tercat Tool & Die Company in a garage at 82 Cedar Street. He outgrew this location and constructed a building at 31 Delaine Street in 1945. The business was engaged in the stamping of jewelry, cosmetics, industrial, commercial coining and premium articles, in base metals, sterling, gold-filled and gold findings. The company, which employed 108 people, distributed its findings, not only in Rhode Island, but also throughout the world. Later, his son, Joseph Terino Jr., became affiliated with his father. Joseph Terino, a graduate of Central High School, is the son of Pasquale Terino, who was born in 1890 in Teano, Italy. Joseph's mother, who was born in 1900 in Naples, Italy, was the former Pasqualina DiGuilio. In 1940, Joseph married Palmina A. (D'Martino) and they were the parents of Joyce Procaccini, Joseph Jr., and Robert Terino. (Courtesy of Gr "Uff" Joseph R. Muratore Collection.)

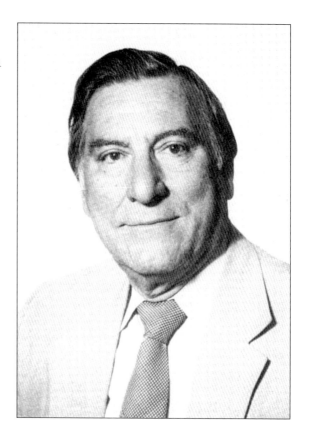

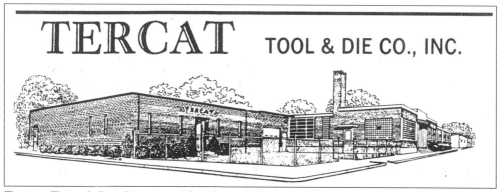

TERCAT TOOL & DIE COMPANY. This photograph shows the business, as it appears today, at 31 Delaine Street, Providence. The building was expanded to its present size in 1984. (Courtesy of Gr "Uff" Joseph R. Muratore Collection.)

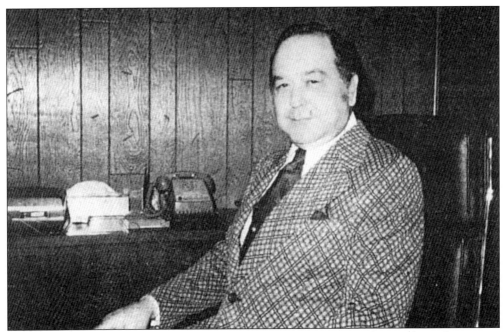

ANTHONY RICCI. Anthony founded the A. Ricci Company, a tool-making and metal-stamping business, in 1944. He was 22 years old when he started, on Admiral Street, in a small, rented shop, which was a 10-by-10-foot room. His tool and die-cutting skills were taught to him by Gino Coletta, and he later completed his skills at the Brown & Sharpe Manufacturing Company. In 1954, he moved to Kinsley Avenue, and in 1968, he moved to his present location at 225 Dean Street, after which his son David joined him in 1974. The business has been engaged in the manufacture of a line of metal findings for jewelry pieces, belt and shoe buckles, and other stamping products. Anthony was born in Providence in 1921, the son of Salvatore and Angelina Ricci. His father owned a barbershop on Federal Hill, near St. John's Church. He married Ellen (Guadagni,) and they became the parents of three children, David A., Glen, and Corrine. (Courtesy of Gr 'Uff' Joseph R. Muratore Collection.)

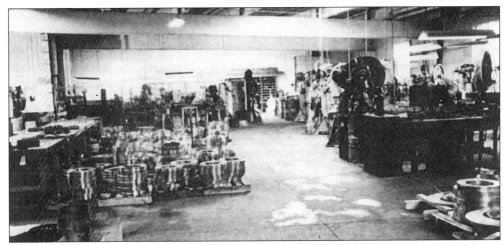

INTERIOR VIEW OF THE A. RICCI INC. STAMPING COMPANY. This company, located at 22 Dean Street, has been in business for 54 years. (Courtesy of Gr 'Uff' Joseph R. Muratore Collection.)

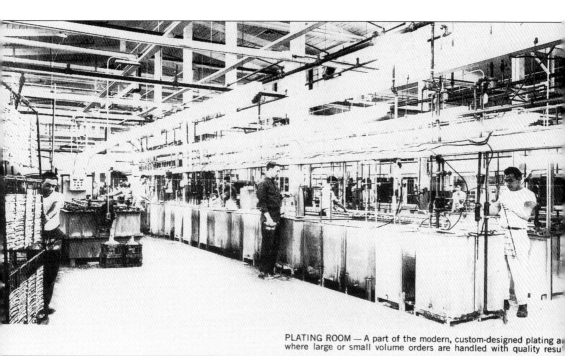

PLATING ROOM — A part of the modern, custom-designed plating a
where large or small volume orders are handled with quality resu

VIEW OF PART OF THE ANTONELLI PLANTING COMPANY. The pictured section of this
modern, custom-designed plating area, was where small or large volume orders for the plating
of metals was carried out. This company was founded by Chris Antonelli and was located on
Valley Street. It employed 200 people in the Providence area. (Courtesy of Gr "Uff" Joseph
R. Muratore Collection.)

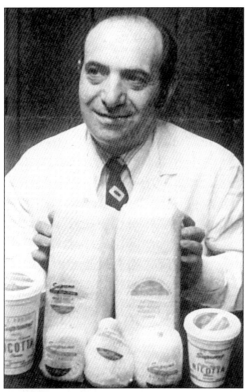

VINCENT BRUZZESE, PRESIDENT OF SUPREME DAIRY PRODUCTS. This dairy business was founded by Vincent's father, Thomas Bruzzesse, who was born in 1891 in Grotteria, Calabria, Italy. Thomas came to America in 1925, and to Rhode Island in 1932, and he married Immacolata (Carabetta,) who was also born in Grotteria. Vincent became part of the business in 1936. In 1940, Providence Cheese Company owned four retail grocery stores in Providence, and one in Boston. In 1950, Vincent formed the Supreme Dairy Farms Company, and sold all the grocery stores. (Courtesy of Gr "Uff" Joseph R. Muratore Collection.)

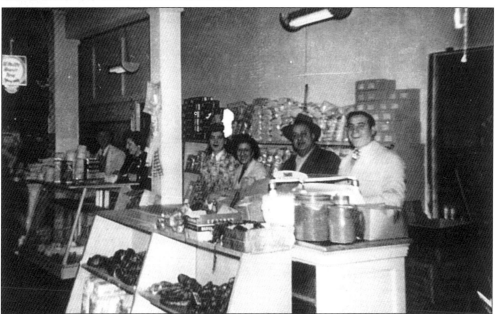

STAFF AND FAMILY MEMBERS AT THE ORIGINAL PROVIDENCE CHEESE STORE. This store was located at 219 Atwells Avenue. To the extreme right of the photograph is Vincent Bruzzese, who managed this and other stores. Vincent, born in 1921 in Grotteria, Italy, attended public schools in Italy and graduated Bridgham Junior High in Providence. Throughout his life he has been a cheese maker. (Courtesy of Gr "Uff" Joseph R. Muratore Collection.)

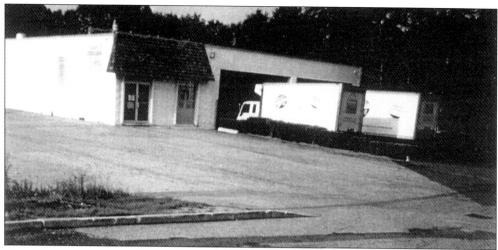

THE WAREHOUSE AND SALES SHOWROOM OF THE SUPREME DAIRY FARMS PLANT. This picture was taken at its present location at 111 Kilvert Street, Warwick. The plant has grown to be one of the largest manufacturers of dairy products in the eastern United States. It now has a cash and carry operation, food service distribution, and store delivery service to super markets and independent food stores in Rhode Island, Massachusetts, New York and Connecticut. The manager of the operation, Vincent Bruzzese, regularly visits cheese plants in Italy, Holland and Denmark. In 1953, he married Ada (Ferraro) in Grotteria, Calabria, Italy, and they became the parents of three children, Thomas Bruzzese Esq., Dr. Anthony Bruzzese, and Richard Bruzzese. (Courtesy of Gr "Uff" Joseph R. Muratore Collection.)

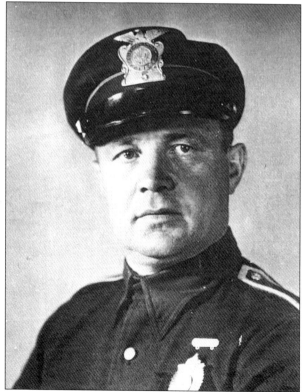

SERGEANT ALBERT N. IZZI. Born in Isneria, Italy, Albert was the son of Olimpio and Maria (Coia) Izzi. He was one of the original four members of the Warwick Police Department, starting as a member of the city's Police Reserve Force. In 1919, he was the first Italian to become a member of the Warwick Police Department. He retired in 1956. Albert was an army veteran of World War I. He played the saxophone and was a member of Irving Berlin's band. He wore his band uniform while serving as a police reserve officer, as the department did not provide uniforms. (Courtesy of Gr "Uff" Joseph R. Muratore Collection.)

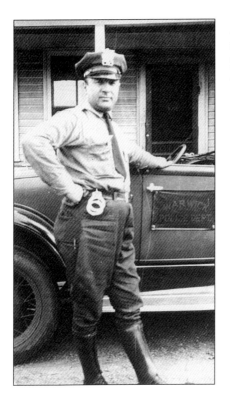

ALBERT N. IZZI WITH HIS AUTOMOBILE. Albert used his own car for police work. He would put signs on when he was on duty. (Courtesy of Gr "Uff" Joseph R. Muratore Collection.)

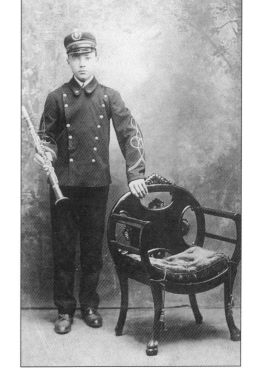

ALBERT N. IZZI AS A YOUNG MAN. After arriving in America, he was drafted and became a member of the army band. He played clarinet and saxophone, and filled in depending on what instrument was needed. (Courtesy of Gr "Uff" Joseph R. Muratore Collection.)

MRS. ALBERT N. IZZI IN 1923. Mrs. Izzi is pictured in front of her and Albert's original grocery store on Central Street in Pontiac. The name Central Street Market later became the Conventry Central Super Market. To the right of this picture is their son, William O. Izzi. Mr. and Mrs. Izzi settled in the Natick section of Warwick, and purchased Medville Farm, which later became Medville Country Club. In 1966, they moved to West Greenwich, where their store, which employed 30 people and was known as Bill Izzi's Supermarket, was on Tiogue Avenue, Coventry. Al Izzi started Al Izzi's Motors in Coventry, a successful business, selling used cars, with an American Motor franchise including Concordes, Gremlins, and Eagles. Both Albert and William operated this business. Albert Izzi Senior, after retiring, became affiliated with all the business operations of his children and helped wherever needed. (Courtesy of Gr "Uff" Joseph R. Muratore Collection.)

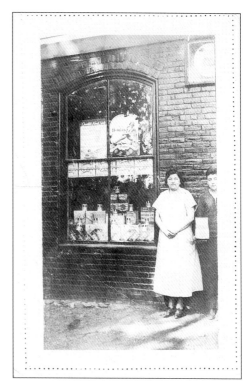

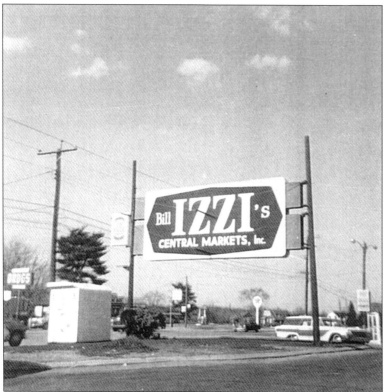

BILL IZZI'S CENTRAL SUPERMARKET ON TIOGUE AVENUE, COVENTRY. A disastrous fire demolished this building. (Courtesy of Gr "Uff" Joseph R. Muratore Collection.)

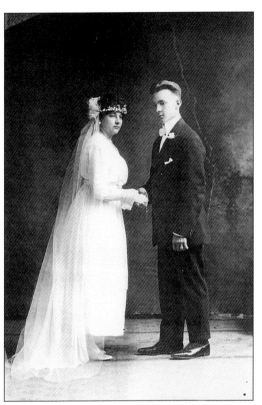

ALBERT N. IZZI AND MARIA C. (LOMBARDI) IZZI ON THEIR WEDDING DAY. They were married on August 7, 1919, and became the parents of four children, William O., who married Arlene Henault; Eva S., who married Anthony Conti, and they had one son, Brian; Albert N., who married Etta Procaccini, and they had one daughter, Genefer; and their first child, Marie Izzi, who became the owner of three beauty salons and gift shops. (Courtesy of Gr "Uff" Joseph R. Muratore Collection.)

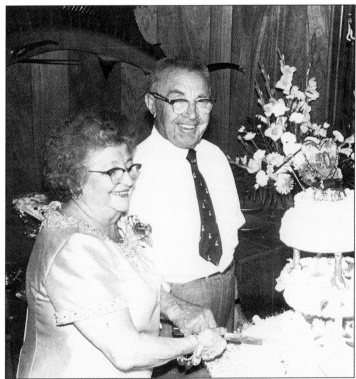

ALBERT N. IZZI AND MARIA C. (LOMBARDI.) The couple is pictured at the celebration of their 50th wedding anniversary. (Courtesy of Gr "Uff" Joseph R. Muratore Collection.)

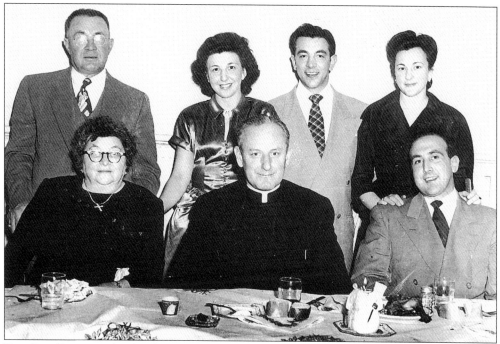

THE IZZI FAMILY. The family, photographed on the 50th wedding anniversary of Albert and Maria, worked together, all involved in each other's activities, always helping each other whenever assistance was required. From left to right, they are, (seated) Maria C. (Lombardi) Izzi, Monsignor John J. Tully, and William O.; (standing) Albert N. Izzi Sr., Eva (Izzi) Conti, Albert N. Jr., and Marie C. Izzi. (Courtesy of Gr "Uff" Joseph R. Muratore Collection.)

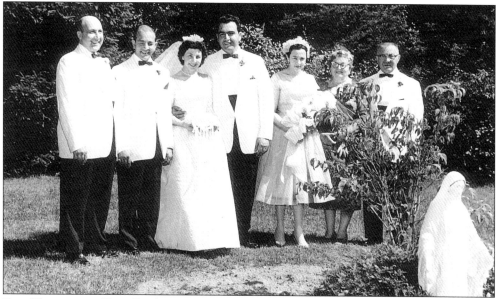

THE WEDDING OF EVA (IZZI) TO ANTHONY CONTI ON SEPTEMBER 12, 1959. Pictured, from left to right, are, William O. Izzi, Albert N. Izzi Jr., Eva (Izzi) Conti, Anthony Conti, Marie C. Izzi, Maria Izzi, and Albert N. Izzi Sr. They were a close-knit, proud, and ambitious family. (Courtesy of Gr "Uff" Joseph R. Muratore Collection.)

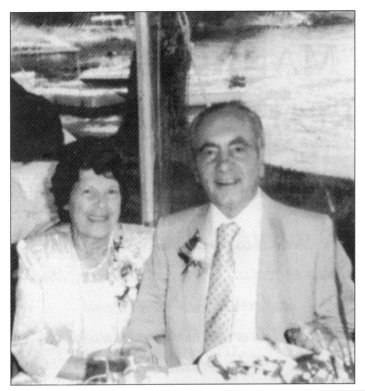

JOHN ASSALONE AND ROSE ASSALONE ON THEIR 50TH WEDDING ANNIVERSARY. In 1939, John married Rose M. (Assane) Assalone. They became the parents of Domenic D., of Evansville, Indiana, and John R., of Coventry, and were the grandparents of seven children. (Courtesy of Gr "Uff" Joseph R. Muratore Collection.)

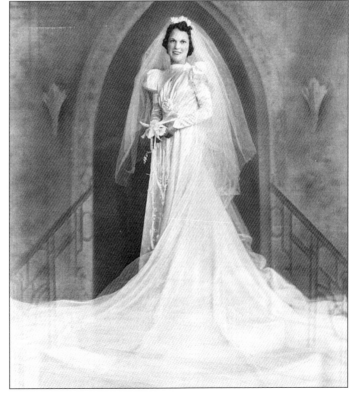

ROSE (ASSANE) ASSALONE ON HER WEDDING DAY, FEBRUARY 5, 1939. Rose married John Assalone in New York in 1939. Later that year they moved to Warwick, R.I. (Courtesy of Gr "Uff" Joseph R. Muratore Collection.)

DOMENICO ASSALONE, FATHER OF JOHN ASSALONE. Domenico came to America with his father, Francesco, when he was 17 years old. He stayed from 1907 until he went back to Italy in 1909. After two years of military service, during which time he became a prisoner of war, Domenico returned, alone, to the United States in 1921. In March of 1924, he brought the rest of the family from Italy, and they settled in Harlem, New York. Domenico was a construction engineer and was killed on his job. (Courtesy of Gr "Uff" Joseph R. Muratore Collection.)

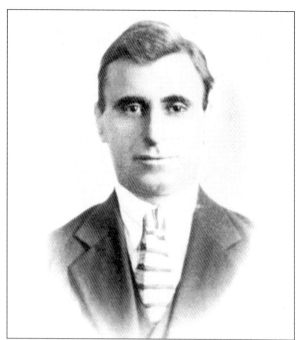

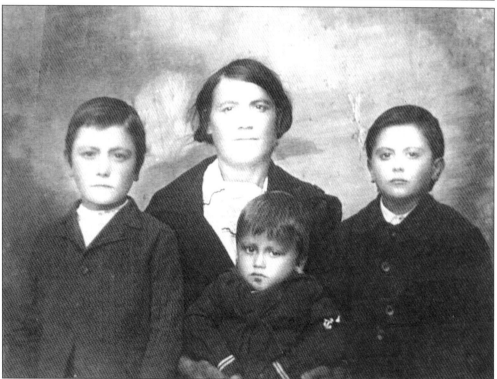

MEMBERS OF THE ASSALONE FAMILY. Pictured, from left to right, are John Assalone, Maria (Del Veccho) Assalone (the mother of John R.), Anthony D. of Warwick, and Frank. They were photographed after John had brought the family to America. (Courtesy of Gr "Uff" Joseph R. Muratore Collection.)

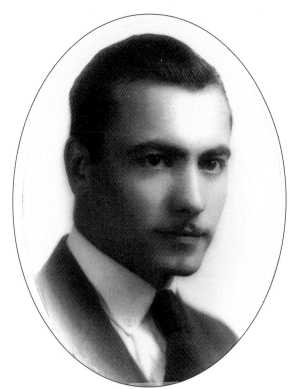

JOHN ASSALONE. He was born in a 13th-century stone house on August 29, 1913, in Gallo Matese, Italy. His life is a story of "It could only happen in America." In 1924, at 11 years old, his father Domenico brought him, his mother, and brother, Frank, to New York City. John had graduated from a one-room schoolhouse. He was a shepherd boy in Gallo. He attended the New York School system, and, as a boy in New York, he worked as a shoe shine boy on Forty-second Street. When John was 17 years old, he lost his father, who was killed in a construction accident. Consequently, John was required to leave school, to help support his mother and brothers. During World War II, he worked at the Walsh Kaiser Shipyard as a foreman. During his spare time, he and his wife grew so much fruit and vegetables that they opened a stand in Warwick, RI. In 1944, John moved his fruit stand into a small building, which had been used as a candy store, and they established a small grocery store, living in the rear room with their two children. Four years later, his wife, and brothers, Frank, Tony and Joe, built a 3,200-square-foot store, calling it Warwick Central Supermarket. It was the first Rhode Island independent supermarket. Following the opening of this store, they opened other stores on Broad Street, Providence, Buttonwoods in Warwick, and Tiogue Avenue in Coventry, and it became Rhode Island's first independent food chain. In 1953, John and Rose moved to Coventry. John created many jobs in Coventry, and he also diversified housing, and helped create a solid tax base. Some of his accomplishments include, the first pre-planned community, the 200-acre Wood Estates, which, when subdivided, created 165 homes; the 100-acre Wood Estates North, creating 150 homes; the first pre-planned open-spaced development, the 100-acre Red Oak Estates, creating 165 homes; and as part of Woodland Manor Housing, the Coventry Health Center, which was the largest nursing home in Rhode Island. All this, he developed with three associates, Antonio Giodano, Dr. Pasquale Confreda, and Ruth Rocchio. They have developed more than 500 acres of land, and, in the process, have created jobs and apartments for Coventry residents, as well as installing Coventry's first sewer line. Today, John is semi retired. He lives at Veronica Court, in Coventry. However, he still goes to his office regularly. (Courtesy of Gr "Uff" Joseph R. Muratore Collection.)

Three

R.I. NOTABLES

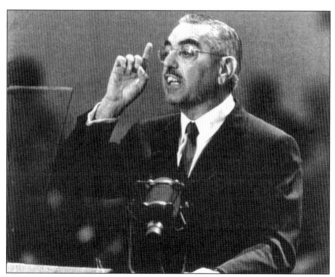

JOHN ORLANDO PASTORE, KEYNOTE SPEAKER, ADDRESSING THE 1964 DEMOCRATIC NATIONAL CONVENTION. In some people's opinion, Pastore had the greatest command of the English language of any person in the United States, and he has been referred to by many journalists throughout the United States as the Jennings Bryan orator of our times. He is a first-generation American of immigrant parents. On October 6, 1945, he became the first Italian governor in Rhode Island. He was also the first Italian senator, and his many appointments to powerful committees in the Senate directly benefited the economy and welfare of Rhode Island. He was chairman of, Atomic Energy; the subcommittee on Textiles; and the subcommittee on Communications. He engineered the legislation for the Kennedy-Nixon television conference at Vienna and Geneva, and he was Senate designee to the Moscow signing of the Neumann Test Ban Treaty. He was floor manager for the Communications Satellite Bill. He has been awarded honorary degrees from over 20 honorary degrees from colleges, even though he did not attend college. He married Elena Elizabeth (Caito) on July 12, 1941, and they became the parents of three children, John Jr. MD, and two daughters, Frances Elizabeth and Louise Marie. (Courtesy of Gr "Uff" Joseph R. Muratore Collection.)

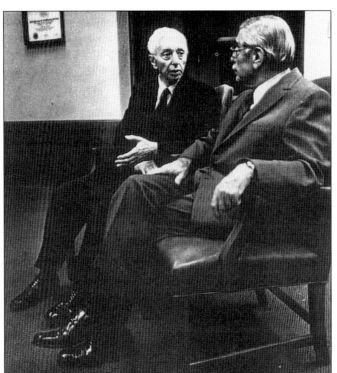

SENATOR JOHN O. PASTORE WITH ADMIRAL HYMAN RICKOVER. Admiral Rickover headed the Atomic Energy project for the United States and was considered the father of the application of atomic energy to the U.S. Navy and submarines. (Courtesy of Gr "Uff" Joseph R. Muratore Collection.)

SENATOR JOHN O. PASTORE ON PRESIDENT JOHN F. KENNEDY'S PRESIDENTIAL YACHT. Senator Pastore is speaking with Senator Edmund Muskie, of Maine, at the America Cup Races, held in 1963, in Newport, RI. (Courtesy of Providence College Archives.)

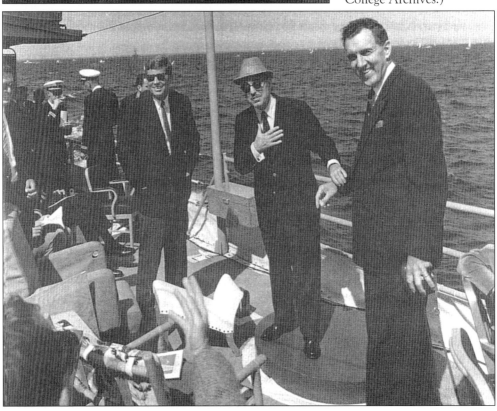

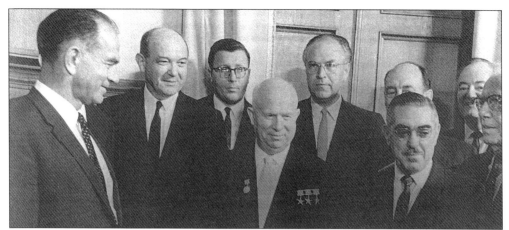

SENATOR JOHN O. PASTORE IN 1963, DURING THE NUCLEAR TEST BAN TREATY NEGOTIATIONS. Also in the photograph are, Premier Nikita Krushchev of Russia, in the center; Secretary of State Dean Rusk; UN Ambassador Adlai Stevenson; and Senators Fulbright, Humphrey, and Aiken. (Courtesy of Providence College Archives.)

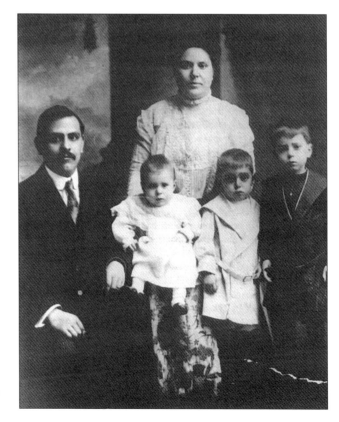

THE PASTORE FAMILY.
Pictured, from left to right, are
Michele Pastore, John's father;
Ermina (Aspirino) Pastore,
John's mother; and their sons,
Lucio, John, and Edmund.
(Courtesy of Gr "Uff" Joseph R.
Muratore Collection.)

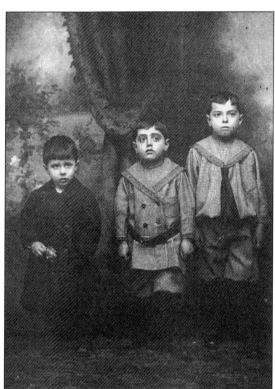

THE PASTORE BROTHERS. Pictured, from left to right, are Edmund, John, and Lucio. (Courtesy of Gr "Uff" Joseph R. Muratore Collection.)

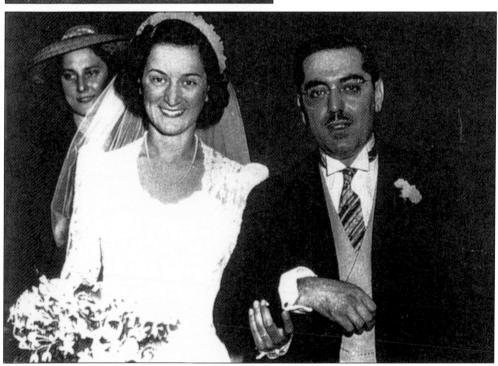

SENATOR JOHN O. PASTORE AND ELENA (CAITO) PASTORE ON THEIR WEDDING DAY, JULY 12, 1941. (Courtesy of Gr "Uff" Joseph R. Muratore Collection.)

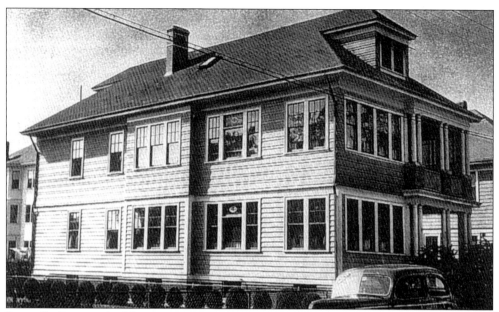

JOHN O. PASTORE'S "EXECUTIVE MANSION." When John and Elena married, they moved to the first floor of this house at 214 Elmdale Avenue in Providence. When he was elected lieutenant governor, this was his "Executive Mansion," from which he conducted the transferal of office, and duties of the office, until an office was provided for him. (Courtesy of Gr "Uff" Joseph R. Muratore Collection.)

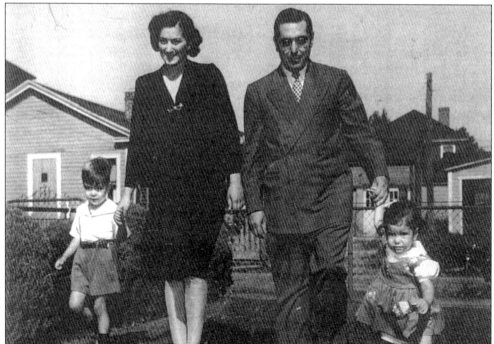

THE PASTORE FAMILY. This photograph of John, Elena, and their children, John Jr. and Frances, was taken shortly after John had become the youngest governor in the U.S. (Courtesy of Gr "Uff" Joseph R. Muratore Collection.)

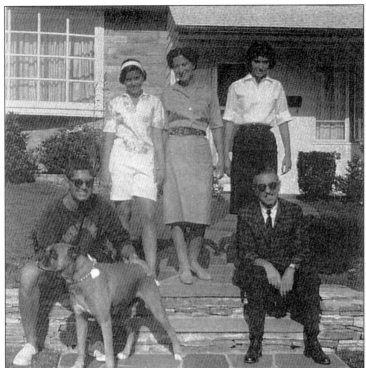

THE PASTORE FAMILY IN FRONT OF THEIR HOME, IN THE GARDEN HILLS SECTION OF CRANSTON. Shown here are, from left to right, as follows: (sitting) son John Jr., Champ the family dog, and John Sr.; (standing) daughter Louise, Elena, and daughter Frances. (Courtesy of Gr "Uff" Joseph R. Muratore Collection.)

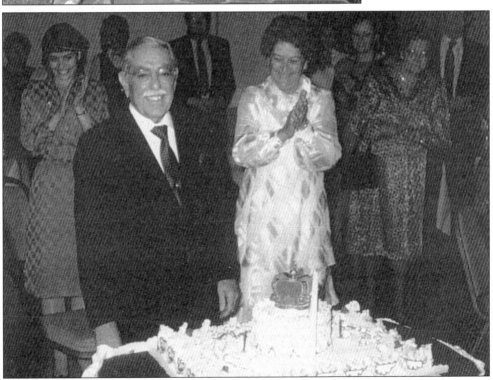

JOHN O. PASTORE AND HIS WIFE, ELENA, ON MARCH 17, 1987, HIS 80TH BIRTHDAY. The party was attended by friends and family. (Courtesy of Gr "Uff" Joseph R. Muratore Collection.)

THE WEDDING DAY OF RAFFAELE CHIODO AND SERAFINA (MILITERNO) CHIODO. They were married on July 18, 1920, at the Holy Ghost Church, Providence. They were the parents of 10 children, of which 8 survived. This family was filled with humility, dignity, and sharing. In two generations, with hard work, planning and sacrifice, their children and grandchildren became lawyers, CPAs, and a head of municipal departments. They elevated themselves, through their efforts and their sacrifices. (Courtesy of Gr "Uff" Joseph R. Muratore Collection.)

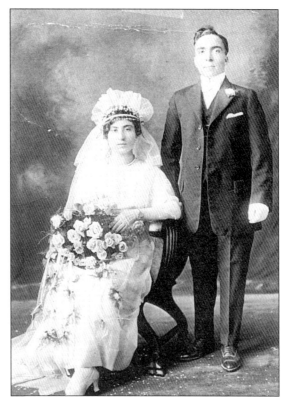

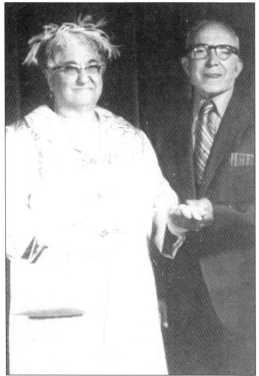

MR. AND MRS. RAFFAELE CHIODO IN 1970. They are pictured on their 50th wedding anniversary, which was attended by their entire family. Raffaele was born on May 25, 1896, in Calabria, Italy. Early in life he realized there was no future for him in his small hometown. He worked at odd jobs to raise enough money in order that he could come to America. In 1910, when he was only 14 years old, he came to America. When he came to Rhode Island to visit friends, he met Serafina, who became his wife. She was born in Cosenza, Italy on October 18, 1897. Raffaele often spoke fondly to his children and grandchildren of his hometown. He would painfully tell them that he could not see a future in Calabria for himself, his children, or his grandchildren. This gave him the courage to come to America for a better life, and for them to have an opportunity to be educated. This was a dream that he saw come true. Raffaele died, in 1988, in his 92nd year. (Courtesy of Gr "Uff" Joseph R. Muratore Collection.)

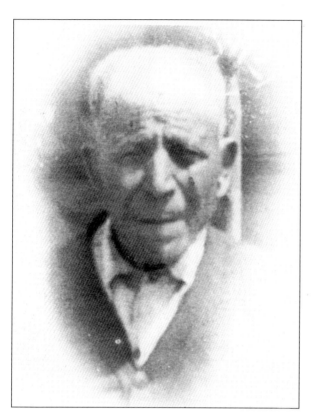

ANTONIO MILITERNO, FATHER OF SERAFINA (FRANCHI) MILITERNO. Antonio was born in Cosenza, Italy, and he came to America, as an adult, to join his family. (Courtesy of Gr "Uff" Joseph R. Muratore Collection.)

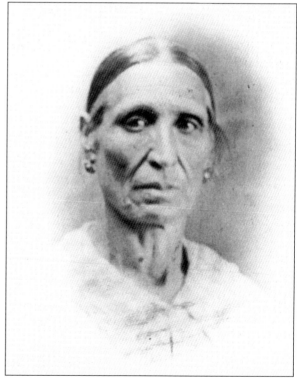

CATERINA (CARDANOME) MILITERNO, MOTHER OF SERAFINA (MILITERNO) CHIODO. Caterina also came to America as an adult. The children sent for their parents in order that they could all live together in America. (Courtesy of Gr "Uff" Joseph R. Muratore Collection.)

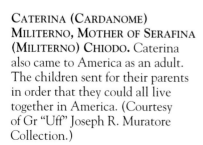

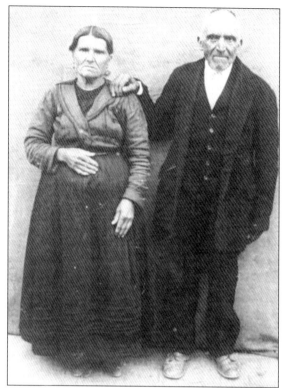

GIUSEPPE AND SERAFINA CHIODO, MOTHER AND FATHER OF RAFFAELE CHIODO. They were both born in San Tommaso Catanzaro, Calabria, Italy, and they came to America in their advanced years to live together with their family. They both died in Providence. (Courtesy of Gr "Uff" Joseph R. Muratore Collection.)

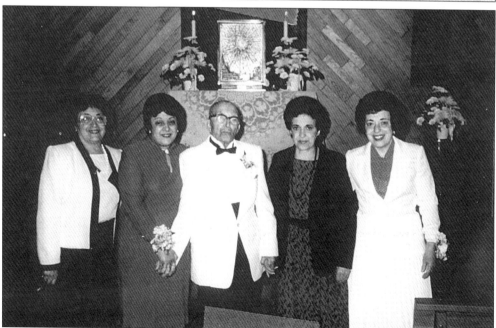

RAFFAELE CHIODO AT HIS 90TH BIRTHDAY PARTY. Raffaele's entire family attended this gathering. Pictured, from left to right, are, Rita (Chiodo) DeLorenzo, Stella (Chiodo) McVeigh, Raffaele Chiodo, Yolanda (Chiodo) Del Conti, and Josephine Chiodo. (Courtesy of Gr "Uff" Joseph R. Muratore Collection.)

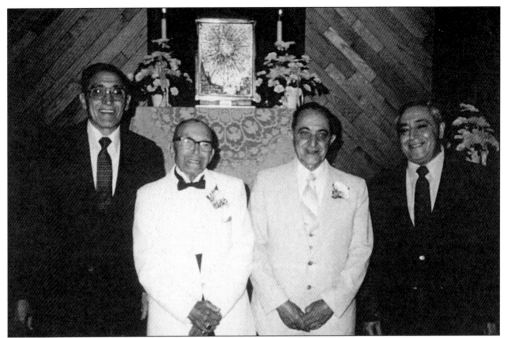

MEN OF THE CHIODO FAMILY. They are pictured at the 90th birthday party of Raffaele Chiodo. From left to right are, Rosario, Raffaele, Emilio, and Luigi. Joseph and Anthony Chiodo were not present for this photograph. (Courtesy of Gr "Uff" Joseph R. Muratore Collection.)

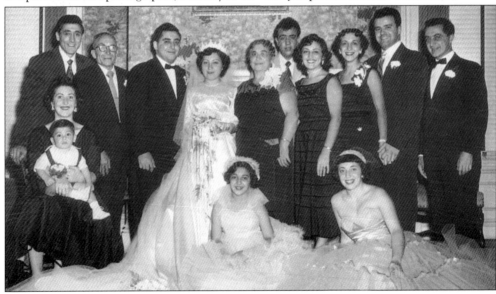

THE ENTIRE CHIODO FAMILY. This photograph was taken on September 19, 1953, on the wedding day of Luigi Chiodo to Elizabeth (Tirelli) Chiodo. Pictured, from left to right, are the following: (seated in the chair) Jean (Rosario's wife) with young Ralph, who is today an attorney and married to attorney Marianne (Santoro) Chiodo; (standing) Rosario; Raffaele; Luigi Chiodo and his wife, Elizabeth (Tirelli); Serafina; Anthony Chodo; Rita; Yolanda Del Conti and her husband, Michael; and Emilio; (seated in the front) Stella and Josephine. (Courtesy of Gr "Uff" Joseph R. Muratore Collection.)

58

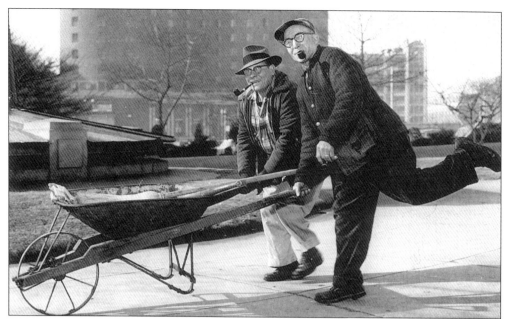

RAFFAELE CHIODO AND A GOOD FRIEND. These two men worked together in the Parks Division for the city of Providence. He was an expert landscaper, caring for trees, grounds and flowers. He retired in 1965, at the age of 72. (Courtesy of Gr "Uff" Joseph R. Muratore Collection.)

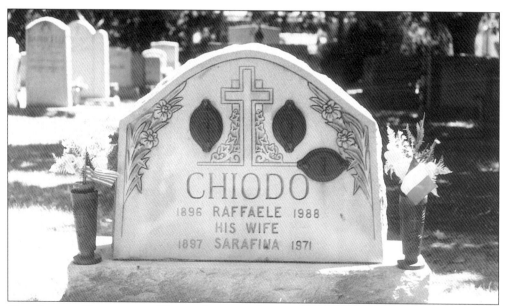

THE CHIODO TOMBSTONE. This tombstone is decorated as Raffaele would have wanted it to be. He never forgot his great love of Italy, and his greatest moment in life, his family tells, was the day he became an American citizen on December 8, 1941. Thereafter, he displayed the American flag discreetly, and whenever he could, with reverence. His children and grandchildren have always, in addition to beautiful flowers, placed a small American and Italian flag on his tombstone. There is no question that the spirit of this humble Italian-American never died. (Courtesy of Gr "Uff" Joseph R. Muratore Collection.)

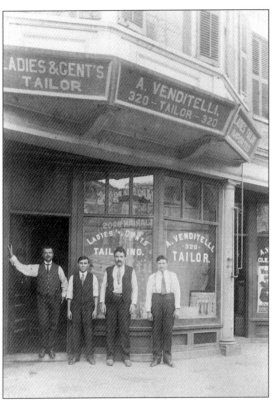

FRANCESCO SCALZO, IN FRONT OF TAILOR SHOP ON CRANSTON STREET. Francesco, pictured second from the right, was employed at this shop in 1906. He immigrated to America in 1900 from Decollatura, Calabria, and he became a life-long resident of Federal Hill until he died in 1953. This is another example of family values and pride, which resulted in one of Francesco's grandsons, Robert J. DeSimone, becoming a regional vice president of Fleet National Bank, as well as the Federal Hill branch for 16 years, from 1980 to 1996, when he retired. (Courtesy of Gr "Uff" Joseph R. Muratore Collection.)

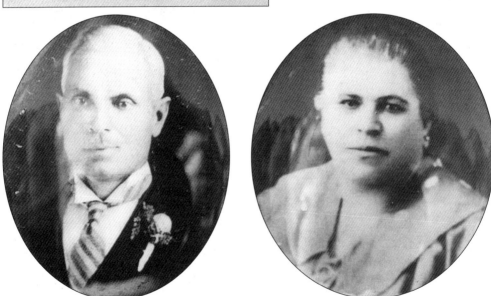

PIETRO DESIMONE AND VINCENZA (SANTAGATA) DESIMONE, GRANDPARENTS OF ROBERT J. DESIMONE, C. 1925. Pietro and Vincenza immigrated to America in 1904 from Naples, and they settled in the Silver Lake section of Providence. They were the parents of seven children, and set values and standards for their children and grandchildren to follow. With their devotion and sacrifices, various members of the family distinguished themselves in the fields of banking, medicine, science, and education. (Courtesy of Gr "Uff" Joseph R. Muratore Collection.)

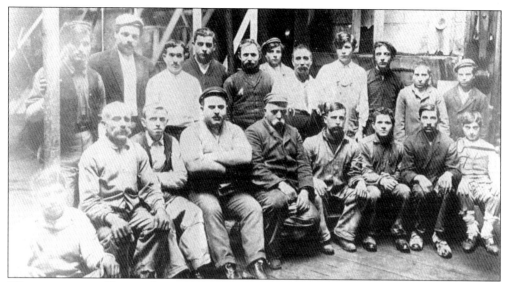

WORKERS AT THE UNITED STATES FINISHING COMPANY, C. 1905. This photograph shows the Queen Branch (Dyers & Bleachers) at 589 Atwells Avenue, Providence. Francesco Scalzo is standing, second from the left. This photograph was taken in the early years, following Franceso Scalzo's arrival to the United States, when he worked at this company for a short time, to provide for his family, until he was able to establish himself in his trade as a tailor. (Gr "Uff" Joseph R. Muratore Collection.)

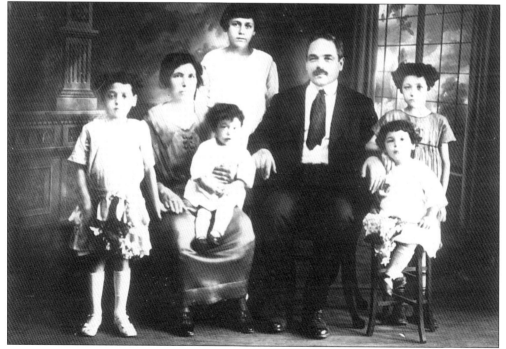

Francesco Scalzo with His Wife Maria, and Five of Their Eleven Children. He became a well-known tailor on Federal Hill, and was able to provide well for his large family. He had developed his skill as a tailor when he was in Italy. (Courtesy of Gr "Uff" Joseph R. Muratore Collection.)

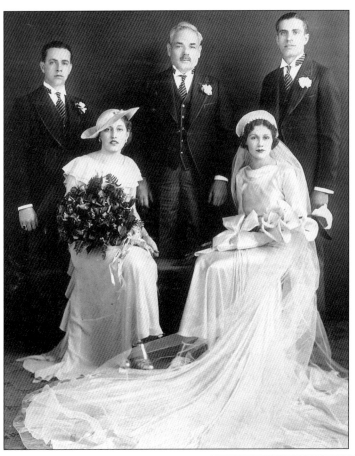

FRANCESCO SCALZO WITH HIS DAUGHTER, ROSE, AND SON-IN-LAW, JOSEPH DESIMONE. This photograph was taken on Rose and Joseph's wedding day on June 8, 1935. Their story reflects the progress made by this family in a short time. Joseph and Rose were the parents of Robert, and Russell, who became a vice president at Analysis & Technology Inc. in Newport, Rhode Island. He married Linda Kraus, and they are the parents of two daughters, Heather and Jennifer. They brought with them values, culture and standards, which, as soon as they were able to establish themselves, they began to display. (Courtesy of Gr "Uff" Joseph R. Muratore Collection.)

THE ROBERT DESIMONE FAMILY IN 1996. A beautiful family blossomed from a humble origin. Robert DeSimone became the regional vice president of Fleet National Bank, supervising 17 branches. Pictured here are the following, from left to right: (seated) Roberta (DelSesto) DeSimone, and the bride, Holly, who married Francesco Ialongo; (standing) Jessica, who married Brian Schattle, Robert, and Rebecca, who married Jose Machado. Mrs. Roberta DeSimone's father was the owner of Louis DelSesto & Son, a wholesaler of fruit and produce, which served all of southeastern New England. (Courtesy of Gr "Uff" Joseph R. Muratore Collection.)

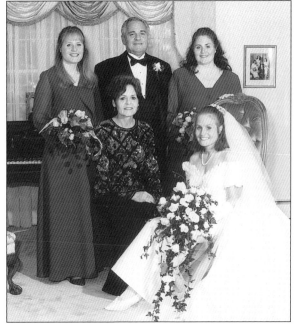

Four

Italian-Americans' Contributions to R.I.

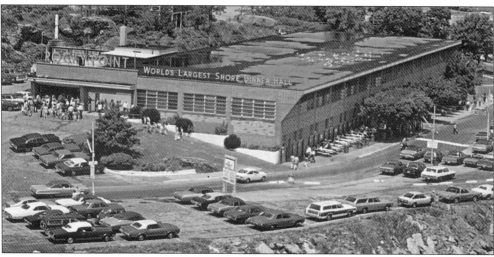

ROCKY POINT PARK, SHORE DINNER HALL. By rotating the seating of guests, 4,000 people could be fed at one time. The dinner hall's clam chowders, clam cakes, lobsters, and shore dinners became known throughout the world. When Conrad Ferla first went to work at Rocky Point, one of his first assignments was manager of the shore dinner hall. It was through his suggestions and insistence that, in 1966, the Windjammer Lounge was added to the Palladium. It became one of the largest dinner halls in Rhode Island, hosting some of the major political and charitable social functions in Rhode Island. It was through Conrad's efforts and hard work that this operation developed to its magnitude and earned Conrad the title of "Mr. Rocky Point." Many Rhode Island state officials, doctors, and lawyers worked at the dinner hall during their college days, to help provide for their tuition. Conrad was proud to point out his many graduates that worked there. (Courtesy of Gr "Uff" Joseph R. Muratore Collection.)

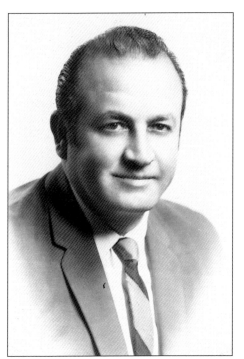

CONRAD FERLA. Conrad was born in 1921 in Siracusa, Sicily, and he died in 1996. He came to America in 1949 and began work for his brother at Rocky Point. He started with no preferential treatment, earning $35 weekly, but, thereafter, his contribution to the phenomenal growth of Rocky Point Park has become history. He was a very valuable community leader, and he was a part of so many charitable organizations in Rhode Island that space does not allow for the inclusion of all his affiliations. However, the following are but a few of the organizations he was active in and an officer of: Big Brothers of Rhode Island; Warwick Businessmen's Association; Warwick Convention Commission; Elks; Warwick Lodge; Kiwanis; American Cancer Society; United Cerebral Palsy; and Rhode Island Commodores. For his services raising funds, and his activities for the Italian-American community, he was named a Cavaleire to the Merit of the Republic of Italy. (Courtesy of Gr "Uff" Joseph R. Muratore Collection.)

CONRAD, AS A YOUNG MAN, WITH THE THEN GENERAL MANAGER OF THE PARK, PAUL HAINEY. This photograph was taken in 1949, in front of the old shore dinner hall. This building was later replaced with the much larger shore dinner hall that existed at the time that the park closed in 1996. (Courtesy of Gr "Uff" Joseph R. Muratore Collection.)

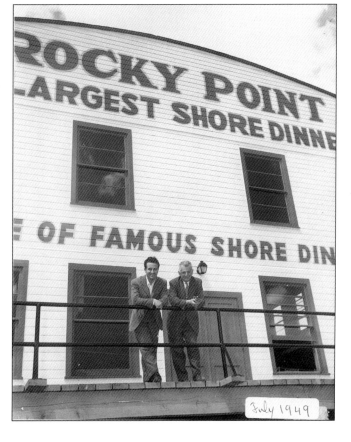

MARIA (FERLA) MALIGNAGGI. Conrad Ferla was the son of Angelica and Sebastiano Angelico Ferla, who were born in Palazzolo Acreide, Sicily. They were the parents of four children: Maria (Ferla) Malignaggi, Vincent, John, and Conrad. Maria married Paul Malignaggi, a violin maker and barber in Sicily. She is the mother of accomplished violinist Joseph Malignaggi (deceased), a graduate of the Julliard School of Music. He was concertmaster and arranger for Frank Sinatra. Maria is 100 years old, and lives in Providence, Rhode Island. (Courtesy of Gr "Uff" Joseph R. Muratore Collection.)

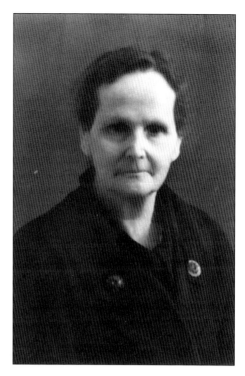

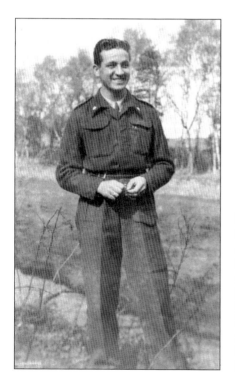

LIEUTENANT CORRADO FERLA, KNOWN AS CONRAD. He was born in Siracusa, Italy in 1921, he died in 1996. He was drafted into the Italian Army in 1941, became a prisoner of war in Africa and sent to Scotland for the balance of the war. While in Scotland, he was allowed to attend the San Salvador College, from which he received a degree. During that time he studied English and when he came to America, he was conversant in the English language. (Courtesy of Gr "Uff" Joseph R. Muratore Collection.)

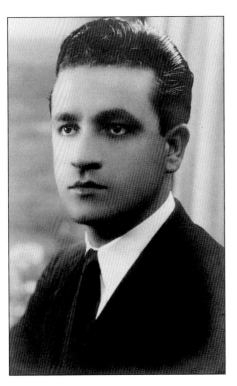

Conrad Ferla married Anita (Cerri) in Italy in 1949, and they were the parents of two children, Alan Robert, who died in 1988, and Conrad Ferla Jr., who died in 1997. Alan married Paula (Maggiacomo), and they were the parents of two children, Carissa Anne, and Alan Robert II. Conrad Ferla Jr. had one son, Conrad Joseph. (Courtesy of Gr "Uff" Joseph R. Muratore Collection.)

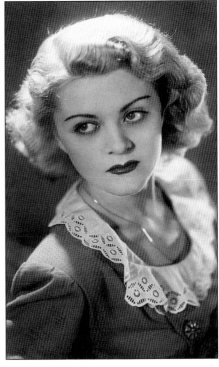

ANITA (CERRI) FERLA, WIFE OF CONRAD. She was born in Milano, Italy, where she attended private college. She received her teacher's diploma from the Infant Mary Magisterium School. In 1950, she came to America. (Courtesy of Gr "Uff" Joseph R. Muratore Collection.)

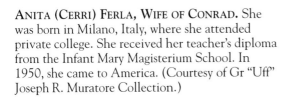

ANITA (RAMELLA) CEPUI,
GRANDMOTHER OF ANITA (CERRI)
FERLA, C. 1940. Anita was born
in Casal-Pusterlengo, Lombardy,
in 1867. She was the mother of six
children, of which, five were sons and
one was a daughter. (Courtesy of Gr
"Uff" Joseph R. Muratore Collection.)

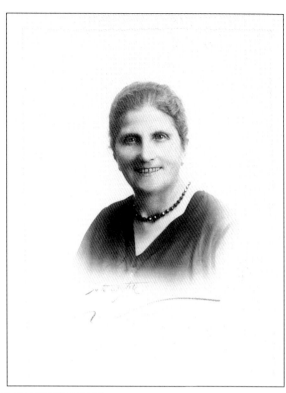

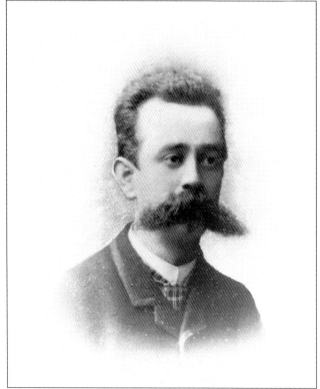

CASARE ANDREA
CERRI, ANITA FERLA'S
GRANDFATHER. He was born
in Castiglione D'Adda in
Lombardy, in 1853. He was
an industrialist, engaged in
the manufacturing of cheese.
(Courtesy of Gr "Uff" Joseph R.
Muratore Collection.)

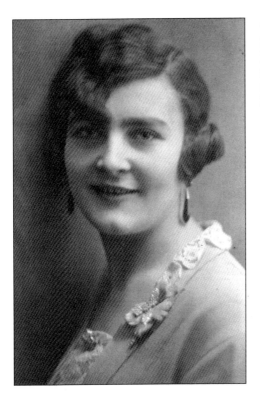

THERESA VALENTINI, MOTHER OF ANITA FERLA. Teresa was born in Ravenna, Emilia, Italy, in 1901. She was an accountant, and she married Cav. Pietro Cerri. Anita was their only child. (Courtesy of Gr "Uff" Joseph R. Muratore Collection.)

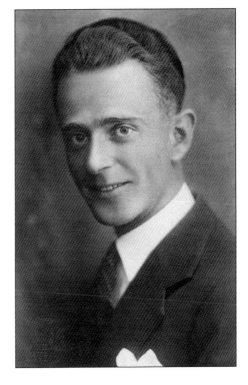

CAVALIERE PIETRO CERRI, FATHER OF ANITA (CERRI) FERLA. Born in Milano, Lombardy, Pietro became an industrialist, engaged in the manufacture and sale of Egyptian cotton. He was decorated twice as Cavaliere, once as a Cavaliere To The Order of Labor, and later as Cavaliere To The Merit Of Vittorio Veneto. He was a veteran of World War I. (Courtesy of Gr "Uff" Joseph R. Muratore Collection.)

THE WEDDING OF CONRAD FERLA AND ANITA (CERRI) FERLA. They were married on December 3, 1949, in the Temple of Athena, Siracusa, Sicily. This temple was built in the seventh century. (Courtesy of Gr "Uff" Joseph R. Muratore Collection.)

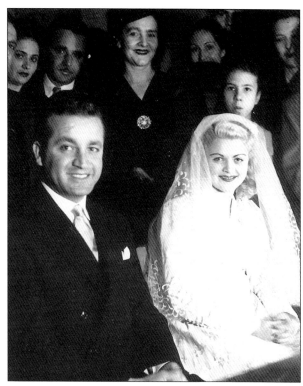

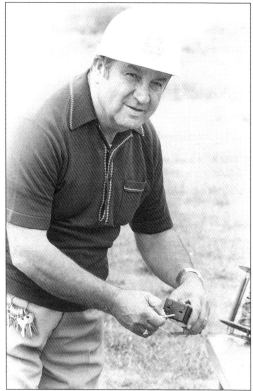

CONRAD FERLA ON AUGUST 10, 1977, ACTIVATING THE DYNAMITE FOR THE BUILDING OF THE "FLUME RIDE." This was one of the largest, most complicated, and expensive fun-making rides at Rocky Point Park, and one of only a few of its kind. Designed and built by a Japanese firm, it was a rollercoaster ride that went through tunnels of water and ended in a waterfall. (Courtesy of Gr "Uff" Joseph R. Muratore Collection.)

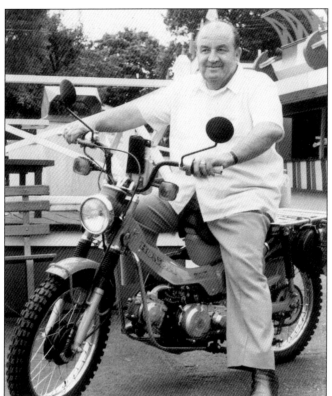

CONRAD FERLA, ON MOTORCYCLE, SUPERVISING ACTIVITIES AT ROCKY POINT PARK. The intense, hands-on supervision that Conrad gave to all the activities at Rocky Point was accomplished by bringing Six motorcycles to the park. They were placed at six strategic locations of the park, and if at any time there was an emergency, either for crowd control, accident or any other reason, Conrad was summoned by two-way radio. He would mount the nearest motorcycle and ride to where his attention was required. This is one of the reasons the park functioned with such efficiency. (Courtesy of Gr "Uff" Joseph R. Muratore Collection.)

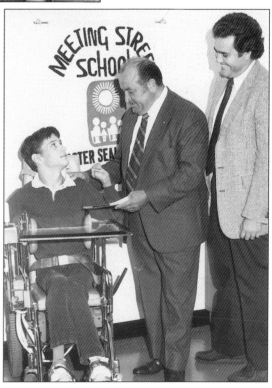

CAVALIERE CONRAD FERLA, C. 1980. He was extremely active in so many charities that space does not allow for them all to be listed. Among his many charities, he sponsored an annual chowder and clambake party for the Meeting Street School children at Rocky Point Park, to which great numbers of handicapped children were brought. The proceeds from the day were donated to the Meeting Street School. (Courtesy of Gr "Uff" Joseph R. Muratore Collection.)

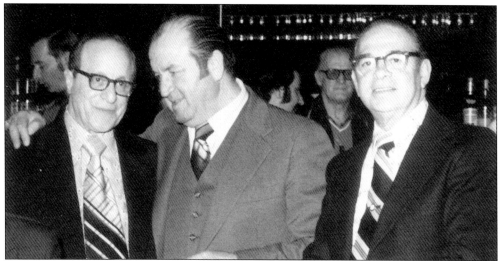

ALDO FREDA ANNUAL CHARITY COMMITTEE MEMBERS, C. 1980. Among the annual parties held at Rocky Point was the Aldo Freda Annual Charity. The proceeds of the event were donated to the needy children of Federal Hill for the purchase of clothing and toys. Conrad was an active member of this committee. Pictured, from left to right, are, Aldo Freda, Conrad Ferla, and John Zuccarrelli. (Courtesy of Gr "Uff" Joseph R. Muratore Collection.)

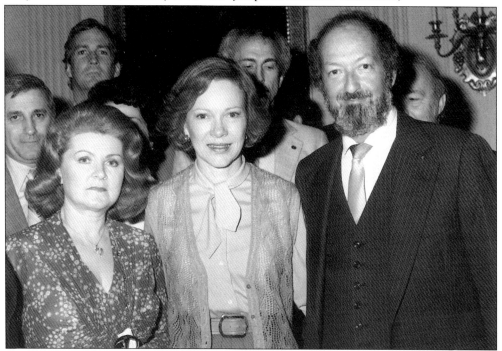

WHITE HOUSE RECEPTION IN WASHINGTON, DC, IN 1978. Conrad participated in so many political, charitable, and fund raising functions that he and Mrs. Ferla were frequently invited as guests to many local, state, and national functions. Pictured, from left to right, are, Mrs. Anita Ferla; First Lady Rosalynn Carter; and Joseph Sinclair, president of the Outlet Company Department Stores and WJAR radio and TV stations. (Courtesy of Gr "Uff" Joseph R. Muratore Collection.)

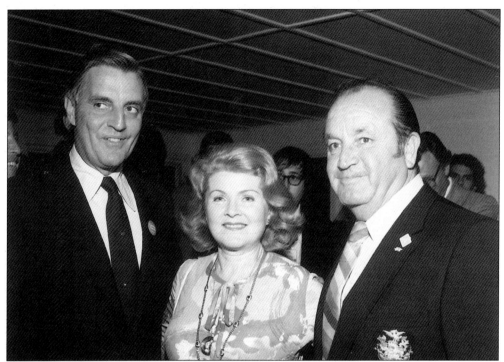

THE ROCKY POINT PALLADIUM, C. 1978. The enormous size of the palladium attracted city, state, and national officials, who were regular visitors. It was an ideal location for large dinners, dances and functions to be held. Pictured, from left to right, are, Vice President Walter Mondale, Mrs. Anita Ferla, and Conrad Ferla. This was one of the many visits that Walter Mondale made to Rocky Point. (Courtesy of Gr "Uff" Joseph R. Muratore Collection.)

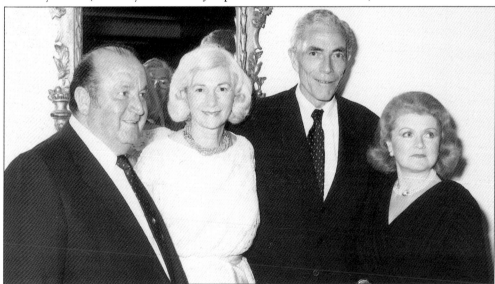

CONRAD, MRS. PELL, SENATOR CLAIBORNE PELL, AND MRS. FERLA AT A RECEPTION IN MAY OF 1983. Senator and Mrs. Pell were the guests of honor at this reception. Through the many visits of Senator and Mrs. Pell to Rocky Point, a strong friendship was developed with the Ferla family. (Courtesy of Gr "Uff" Joseph R. Muratore Collection.)

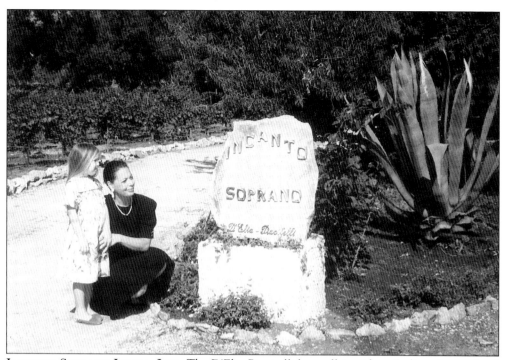

INCANTO SOPRANO ITALIA, LTD. The D'Elia-Piacitelli love affair with an Italian vineyard and olive grove blossomed in 1972, and has now become a reality. Incanto Soprano is the name of a company, incorporated in Rhode Island, that translates as "High Enchantment." This company has its roots in Francavilla, near Brindisi, in the southeasterly section of the peninsula or boot area of Italy, on the Adriatic side. Some of the olive trees on this estate are 300 years old, others are 600 years old, and one tree is 1,000 years old. From the olives of these trees is produced some of the finest olive oil in Italy. The age of these trees was established by a test called the olific oil test, which measures the acid content of the oil. The older a tree, the less acid it contains, which gives olive oil a smooth, clear taste and aroma. The courtship started when William Piacitelli and Mary Ellen Pompii D'Elia Piacitelli visited the estate in 1972. William fell in love with the scenery, the nearness to the Adriatic Sea, and the unusual design and construction of the Truollo-style buildings in the area and on the estate. He also admired the rooftop turrets of stone, which had been built hundreds of years ago by local Italian tribes before communities were established. When William and Mary Ellen tasted the various wines and oils produced on the estate, they decided they wanted to become part of this homeland, farmland production. Soon thereafter, they made arrangements to purchase part of the land, and on their return to America, they organized the company under Rhode Island laws. Gradually, Bill and Mary Ellen began to modernize the home and the equipment at the estate. They brought more electrical power to the area, they had driven wells installed, and they modernized the buildings, the plumbing, and the courtyards. Local craftsmen were engaged, as well as experts to prune the trees and begin the production of the oil and wines. Each summer, between June and September, Mary Ellen and their daughter, Eden, spend these months in Italy, supervising and conducting the affairs of business, and its expansion for the following year. Eden is now 11 years old, and speaks Italian flawlessly. Bill and Mary Ellen have given all the wines melodious-sounding names, and one of their wines was named Eden, after their daughter. Some of the other names they have given to the wines are Saggio, Primitivo, and Valeria. Their on-site supervisor at the estate is a cousin of Mary Ellen, Giuseppe D'Elia, who is a college professor during the school year. He supervises the affairs of the estate, as Mary Ellen and Bill live in Rhode Island. (Courtesy of Gr "Uff" Joseph R. Muratore Collection.)

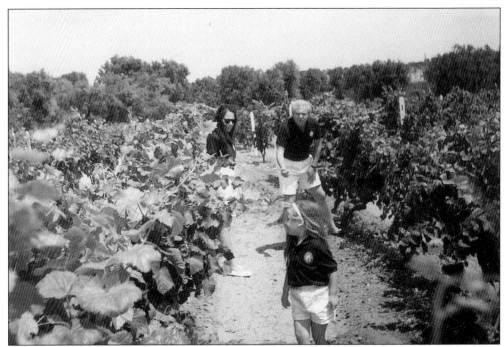

A Well-Cropped, Well-Spaced Grape Vineyard and Olive Grove. Pictured, from left to right, are, Mary Ellen D'Elia Piacitelli, William Piacitelli, and their daughter Eden, c. 1997. From this olive grove, the first press, cold press, extra virgin olive oil is produced. (Courtesy of Gr "Uff" Joseph R. Muratore Collection.)

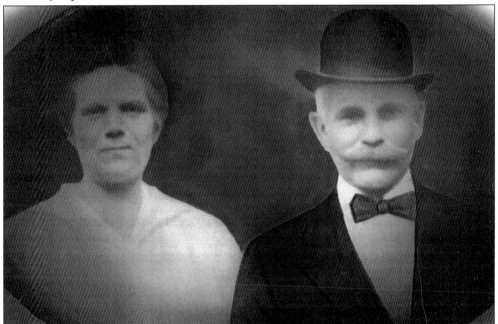

Gulia Molla and Costantino Piacitelli, c. 1902. This couple came to America in 1910. They were the grandparents of Willaim Piacitelli. (Courtesy of Gr "Uff" Joseph R. Muratore Collection.)

GIUSEPPE D'ELIA AND CARMELLA (GRANIERI) D'ELIA. They were married on November 10, 1912, and they became the parents of seven children, of which four were boys and three were girls. Giuseppe came to the United States in 1896, alone, at the age of 16. They are the grandparents of Mary Ellen D'Elia Piacitelli. (Courtesy of Gr "Uff" Joseph R. Muratore Collection.)

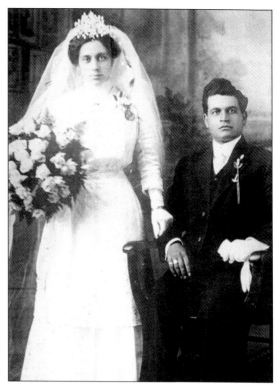

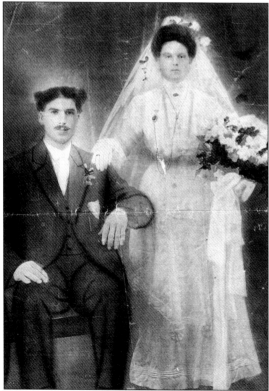

CRESCENZO POMPEII AND MARIA POMPEII ON THEIR WEDDING DAY, DECEMBER 12, 1909. Crescenzo and Maria were both from Frosenone, Italy. They were the parents of six children, and the paternal grandparents of Mary Ellen D'Elia Piacitelli. When they came to America, Crescenzo was employed at the Barrington Brick Works for many years. (Courtesy of Gr "Uff" Joseph R. Muratore Collection.)

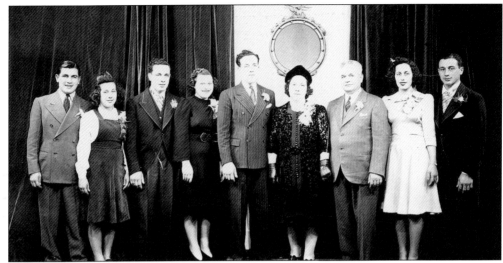

FAMILY PHOTOGRAPH OF THE POMPII-D'ELIA CHILDREN, AS ADULTS. These are the children of Giuseppe and Carmella Granieri D'Elia. From left to right, they are, Damian D'Elia, Mary D'Elia Jenkins, Leonardo D'Elia, Angela D'Elia Pompeii, Pietro D'Elia, Carmella Granieri D'Elia, Giuseppe D'Elia, Felicia D'Elia Asadoorian, and Cosimo D'Elia. (Courtesy of Gr "Uff" Joseph R. Muratore Collection.)

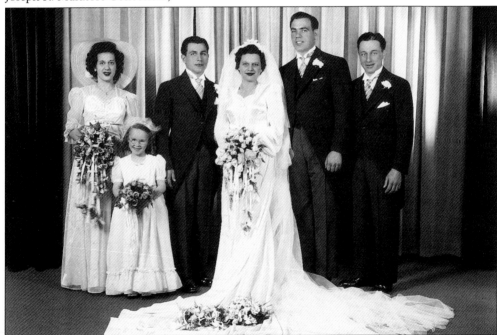

THE WEDDING OF JOHN POMPEII AND ANGELA D'ELIA POMPEII, APRIL 27, 1946. John was the founder of the Modern Trucking Company Riggers. They were the parents of one child, Mary Ellen D'Elia Piacitelli. It was at the strong persuasion by Angela D'Elia Pompeii to her daughter, that Mary Ellen D'Eia Piacitelli visited the family estate in Francavilla, Brindisi, Italy. Pictured, from left to right, are, Mary D'Elia Jenkins, flower girl Patricia D'Elia, Damian D'Elia, Angela D'Elia Pompeii, John Pompeii, and Cosimo D'Elia. (Courtesy of Gr "Uff" Joseph R. Muratore Collection.)

THE WEDDING OF MICHELENA "LENA" NAPOLITANO AND GAETANO "GUY" EDMUND PIACITELLI. They were married in February, 1939, and were the parents of William Piacitelli. Also in the photograph are Mary "Dolly" Battista and Dominic "Gabe" Crocenzi. (Courtesy of Gr "Uff" Joseph R. Muratore Collection.)

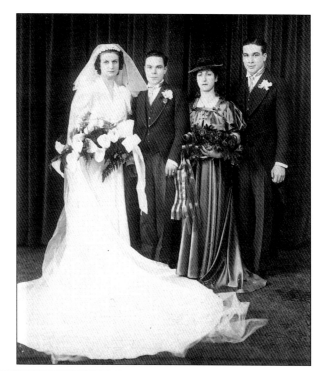

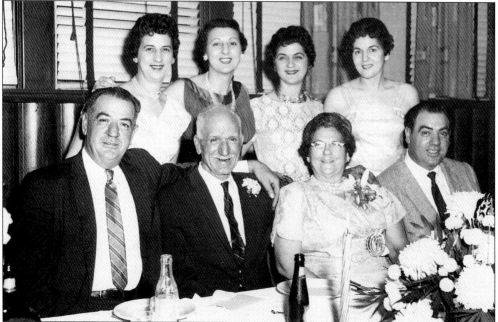

THE 50TH WEDDING ANNIVERSARY OF CRECENZO POMPEII AND MARIA CIOE POMPEII, IN 1959. Luigi and Maria were the paternal grandparents of Mary Ellen D'Elia Piacitelli. Shown in this photograph, from left to right, are, (seated) Luigi Pompeii, Crescenzo Pompeii, Maria Cioe Pompeii, and John Pompeii; (standing) Barbara Pompeii Lomastro, Filomena Pompeii D'Elia Oliva, Anna Pompeii Florenzano, and Angela Pompeii Acciardo. (Courtesy of Gr "Uff" Joseph R. Muratore Collection.)

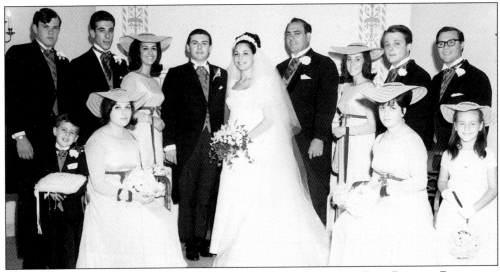

THE WEDDING OF WILLIAM A. PIACITELLI AND MARY ELLEN D'ELIA POMPEII PIACITELLI ON AUGUST 27, 1966. William and Mary Ellen are the founders of the Incanto Soprano Italia Vineyard and Olive Groves. Mary Ellen is the president of the corporation. Pictured, from left to right, are, (front row) Joseph Rodreguies Jr., (seated) Claire D'Elia, Anna DiNitto-D'Elia Jr, and Mary Ann Jenkins Willis; (back row) Robert Swenson, Anthony Crocenzi, Donna Sormanti Sagglio, William A. Piacitelli, Mary Ellen D'Elia Pompeii Piacitelli, John Pompeii, Judy Romano Ferra, Paul Capice, and Roland Antonelli. (Courtesy of Gr "Uff" Joseph R. Muratore Collection.)

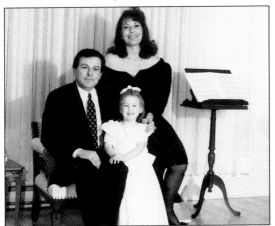
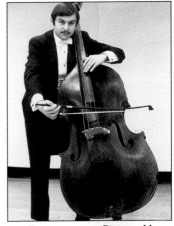

LEFT: THE PIACITELLI-D'ELIA FAMILY, 1990, IN THEIR HOME IN PROVIDENCE. Pictured here are William A. Piacitelli, his wife, Mary Ellen D'Elia Pompeii Piacitelli, and their daughter Eden Angela D'Elia Pompeii Piacitelli. (Courtesy of Gr "Uff" Joseph R. Muratore Collection.)
RIGHT: WILLIAM A. PIACITELLI, FOUNDER OF INCANTO SOPRANO ITALIA LTD. William, pictured here in 1967, played as the principal double bassist with the Louisville Orchestra, the Boston Pops, the Rhode Island Philharmonic, the Milwaukee Symphony, and the North Carolina Symphony. He was a member of the faculty of the University of Rhode Island, and in 1967, he was on the staff of the Louisville School of Music. He has taught at Brown University, University of Rhode Island, Rhode Island College, and Barrington University. He was also the founder of William's Restaurant in Providence, and United Wines Limited. (Courtesy of Gr "Uff" Joseph R. Muratore Collection.)

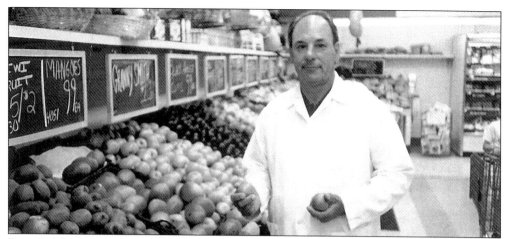

DAVE'S MARKETPLACE. David Cesario, founder and owner of Dave's Marketplace, was born in the Federal Hill section of Providence, in 1943, at the corner of Swiss and Courtland Streets. He attended local schools in Providence, and graduated from Brigham Junior High. He attended Central High School for only 12 days, and, when he left, he obtained his working papers and went to work at a chemical factory for three years. He worked at various jobs that were neither challenging nor fulfilling to him, until he opened a small fruit stand, in 1971, on West Shore Road in Warwick. He now owns five of the largest supermarkets, and owns the largest chain of independent supermarkets in Rhode Island. He employs more than 560 people, the majority of which are high school and college students. He now has an annual sales volume of more than $46 million. He is truly an example of an American dream come true.

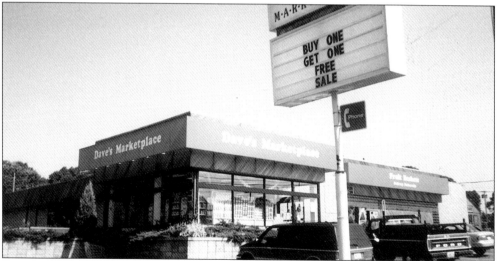

DAVE'S MARKETPLACE AT 2687 WEST SHORE ROAD, WARWICK. This was the first supermarket he built, directly across the street from his original small shed-like fruit stand. He added to this store many times and now it is one of the nicest stores in the area. It was through Dave's enterprising promotional ideas of "buy one get one free," that Dave's concept of mass marketing developed at this original store, and now it is used at all his stores. Due to the tremendous purchasing power that has now been developed at Dave's stores, the freshest fruits and vegetable of the highest quality are received daily in his markets, from all over the world, including Australia, Israel, South America, and Mexico. (Courtesy of Gr "Uff" Joseph R. Muratore Collection.)

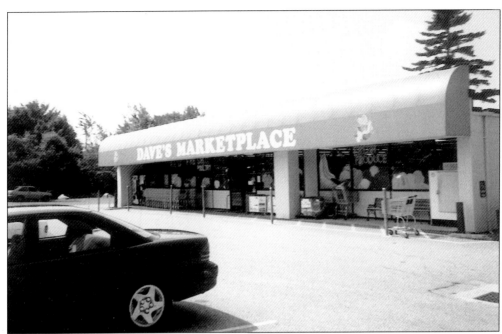

DAVE'S MARKETPLACE AT 4 CEDAR SWAMP ROAD, GREENVILLE, R.I. This was store number 2. It was established in 1976, in an area that contained highly competitive markets, but due to Dave's marketing ability and the store's cleanliness and wide variety of food products, the store succeeded, and today is one of the finest stores in the area. (Courtesy of Gr "Uff" Joseph R. Muratore Collection.)

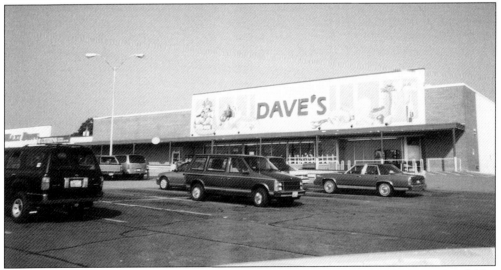

DAVE CESARIO'S THIRD STORE, OPENED IN 1994. This store is located at 5941 Post Road, No. Kingstown, formerly occupied by the Almacs supermarket. This supermarket, as with his other stores, has full and complete departments for fish, meats, groceries, fruits, delicatessen, and gourmet foods. The location of the store is in one of the fastest growing areas in South County. Due to his enormous sales volume, Dave's bakes its own pastry and breads, cuts and packages its own meats, and also cuts, packages, and prepares a large assortment of fish products of every kind. (Courtesy of Gr "Uff" Joseph R. Muratore Collection.)

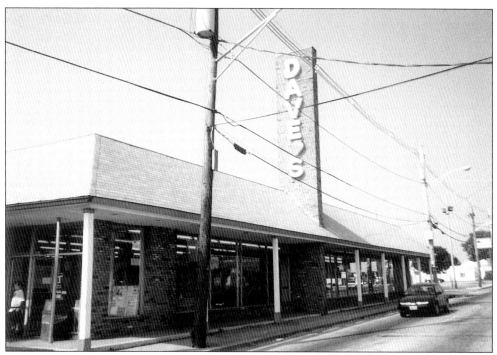

DAVE'S FOURTH STORE, LOCATED AT 18 AIRPORT ROAD, WARWICK. This building formerly housed Almacs Hoxie Supermarket. When Dave opened this location, it was enthusiastically received by the community and surrounding areas. It serves a definite need, as a market of this size was needed in such a central location. One of the features of this store was naming aisles for major streets in the area, such as Warwick Avenue, West Shore Road, and Hoxie. This sparked conversation and added to the friendly atmosphere of the store. While this book was being written, a fifth store was opened at 125 Tower Hill Road, Wickford, in a unique and picturesque area that is within a short distance of the oceanfront. (Courtesy of Gr "Uff" Joseph R. Muratore.)

DAVE'S MATERNAL GRANDFATHER, ANDREW DI IORIO. He was born in Iscia, Naples, and he came to America in 1907. (Courtesy of Gr "Uff" Joseph R. Muratore Collection.)

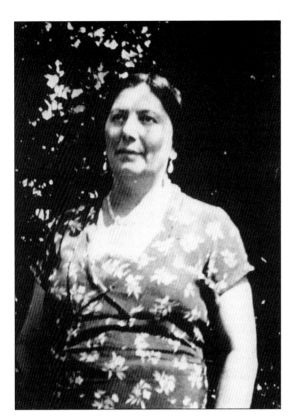

GENOVEFFA (ARDITO) DI IORIO, DAVE CESARIO'S MATERNAL GRANDMOTHER, C. 1932. She was born on May 26, 1886, the daughter of Elizabeth (Torzi) Ardito and Antonio Ardito. Genoveffa was the mother of eight children, Joseph, Albert, Gicondina, Mario, Delphine (Dave's mother) Anne, William, and Gino. (Courtesy of Gr "Uff" Joseph R. Muratore Collection.)

VARIOUS MEMBERS OF DAVE'S FAMILY, 1955. Pictured in this photograph, from left to right, are, Sue Menard, Dave's paternal aunt; Albert Cesario, Dave's paternal grandfather; and Julia Cesario, his father's sister. (Courtesy of Gr "Uff" Joseph R. Muratore Collection.)

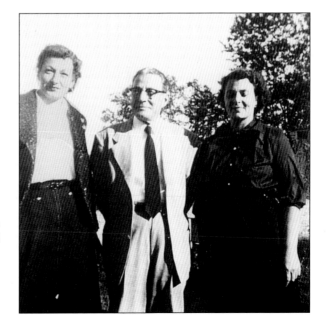

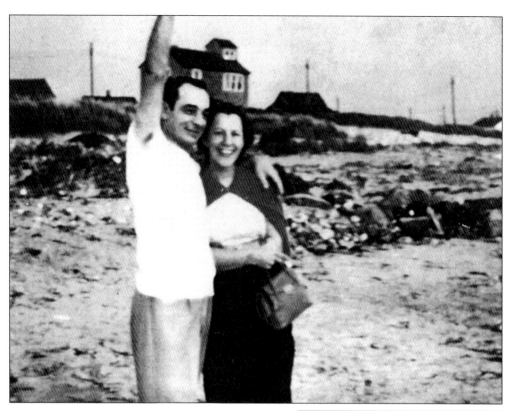

DAVE CESARIO WITH HIS MOTHER, DELPHINE (DI
IORIO) CESARIO, IN 1958. Dave's family has always
been a close-knit unit. His father, Arelio Cesario,
died in 1971. His mother died in 1974. (Courtesy of
Gr "Uff" Joseph R. Muratore Collection.)

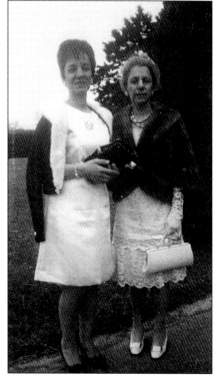

DELPHINE (DI IORIO) CESARIO (DAVE'S MOTHER)
AND ANNE CESARIO (DAVE'S MATERNAL AUNT),
c. 1968. Delphine died in 1974. (Courtesy of Gr
"Uff" Joseph R. Muratore Collection.)

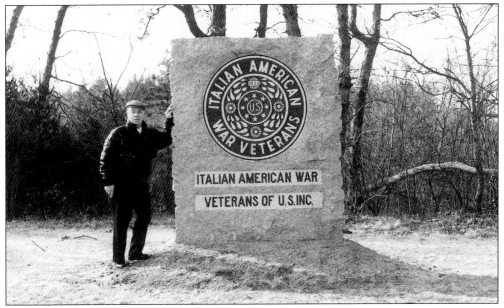

DANDO DIMANNA AT THE ITALIAN AMERICAN WAR VETERANS MONUMENT. This was erected at the Veterans Cemetery in Exeter, Rhode Island, on a 110-acre parcel of land. It was an idea conceived by Dando DiManna and, after much effort,, he was able to have this boulder donated, brought into place, and inscribed. Friends of the veterans carried out most of the work. The first burial in Exeter was in 1975, and today there are more than 14,000 veterans buried there, of which 200 are "Missing In Action" (MIA) plots. These plots have no remains, only a regulation marker with the MIA person's name inscribed on it where family and relatives visit to pray. (Courtesy of Gr "Uff" Joseph R. Muratore Collection.)

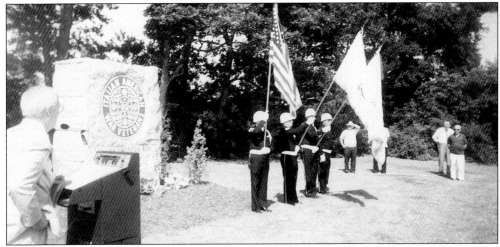

SENATOR VINCENT BACCARRI'S DELIVERY SPEECH AT THE DEDICATION CEREMONY OF THE ITALIAN AMERICAN WAR VETERANS OF THE UNITED STATES MONUMENT. This monument was erected in honor of veterans of all wars who may be buried there. National attention has been given to this cemetery, for the dignity, high respect, and honor paid to the veterans who are buried here, as well as for the excellent maintenance of the beautiful grounds. Shown in the photograph is the Honor Guard of the Italian-Americans World War II Veterans. (Courtesy of Gr "Uff" Joseph R. Muratore Collection.)

Five

DISTINGUISHED R.I. ITALIAN AMERICANS

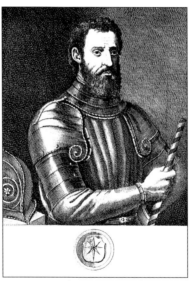

GIOVANNI DA VERRAZZANO, FROM AN ANCIENT WOOD ETCHING. Giovanni was an Italian mariner of the 16th century who discovered and charted the Narragansett Bay region and the entire East Coast area of North America. The Verrazzano Observance Day Committee, of The Grand Lodge Of Rhode Island Order Sons Of Italy, and the Department Of The Rhode Island Italian-American War Veterans of the United States, established, in 1961, a fund to annually honor a Rhode Islander. The process of selection for the Verrazzano Day Award was to choose an individual of Italian origin, who, through their achievements, efforts and dedication to the state, had made a significant contribution in helping Italian-Americans in the furtherance of their endeavors. The fund was created in honor of Giovanni, for establishing an area where tranquillity and peace prevailed, and where our ancestors could find a peaceful home. (Courtesy of Gr. "Uff" Joseph R. Muratore Collection.)

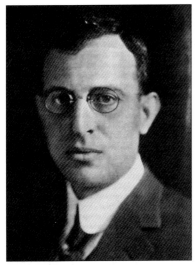

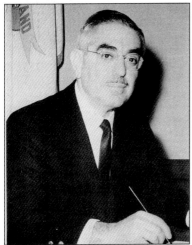

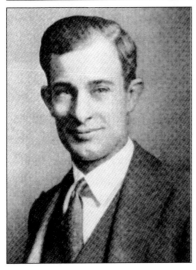

TOP PHOTOGRAPH: ANTONIA CAPOTOSTO, 1962 RECIPIENT, ASSOCIATE JUSTICE OF THE SUPREME COURT. Antonio came to R.I. in 1905 and settled on Federal Hill. He was the first Italian lawyer, and the first Harvard graduate of Italian birth. He was born in Caprriati al Voltunno, in Campobasso, Italy, in 1879, the son of Luigi and Enrichetta (R'Orsi) Capotosto. He obtained his law degree in 1904, and was appointed an Associate Justice of the Supreme Court from 1922 to 1935., when he was appointed an Associate Justice of the Rhode Island Supreme Court. The Royal Crown of Italy named him Cavaliere in 1924. he died on December 3, 1962. (Courtesy of Gr "Uff" Joseph R. Muratore Collection.)

MIDDLE PHOTOGRAPH: JOHN O. PASTORE, 1963 RECIPIENT, LAWYER, LEGISLATURE, GOVERNOR, AND STATESMAN. Born in Providence on March 17, 1907, the son of Michele and Erminia (Asprinio) Pastore, he attended Classical High School and graduated from Northeastern University Law School in 1931. He was elected to the House of Representatives in 1934, serving until 1937, when he was appointed Assistant Attorney for the State of Rhode Island. In 1939 he was elected Lieutenant Governor, then Governor, and in 1950 he was elected to the Senate. He served as the chairman of the Joint Committee of Congress on Atomic Energy and was the chairman of the Subcommittee of Communications. He was also instrumental in creating the Communications Satellite Bill, which made possible the development of world-wide television by Telstar, Syncom, and other satellites. He is considered by many to be one of the greatest orators of our time, and was the keynote speaker for the National Democratic Convention that nominated Lyndon B. Johnson to become the Presidential candidate. He married Elena Elizabeth (Caito) Pastore; they had three children, John Fr., Frances Elizabeth, and Louise Marie. (Courtesy of Gr "Uff" Joseph R. Muratore Collection.)

BOTTOM PHOTOGRAPH: LOUIS W. CAPPELLI, 1964 RECIPIENT. Louis was born in Providence on April 14, 1894, the son of Antonio and Maria (Pettine) Cappelli. He was a graduate of LaSalle Academy, Brown University, and Yale Law School. During World War I, he served in the United States Army. In 1932, Louis was elected secretary of state, and in 1934, he was named Associate Justice of Rhode Island Supreme Court. He was married on June 16, 1923, to Catherine McQuade, and they were the parents of six children, Louis W. Jr., Anthony Francis, Thomas Albert, C. Edward, Mary Anna, and John. (Courtesy of Gr "Uff" Joseph R. Muratore Collection.)

THOMAS J. PAOLINO, 1965 RECIPIENT.
Thomas was born on December 14, 1905.
After graduating Brown University, he
attended Harvard Law School. In 1956,
he was named Associate Justice of Rhode
Island Superior Court. He was a writer on
zoning matters. He retired from court in
1978. Thomas married Florence (Dolice,)
and they were the parents of three children.
(Courtesy of Gr "Uff" Joseph R. Muratore
Collection.)

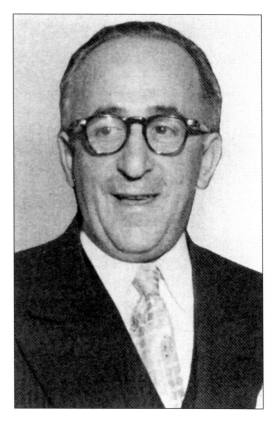

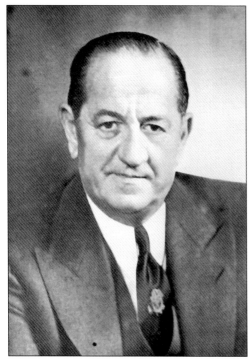

**CAVALIERE VINCENT SORRENTINO, 1966
RECIPIENT, MANUFACTURER, AND CIVIC
LEADER.** Vincent was born in Castellamare
di Stavia, Naples, on February 22, 1891, the
son of Luigi and Anna (Caruso) Sorrentino
of the island of Ischia. He immigrated to
America in 1906, and in 1911, he founded
Uncas Manufacturing Company at 9
Calendar Street, Providence. This company
became the world's largest ring manufacturer,
and at one time, he employed 800 people.
Vincent was active in numerous charitable
and business organizations. In 1962, he
was decorated by the Italian government,
and named a Cavaliere to the Merit of the
Republic of Italy. In 1911, he married Katie
(Goldenstein,) and they were the parents
of seven children, Ann Marie, Loretta
Louisa, Helena Evelyn, Dorothy Edna,
Louis Vincent, Gloria Virginia, and Stanly
Lawrence. (Courtesy of Gr "Uff" Joseph R.
Muratore Collection.)

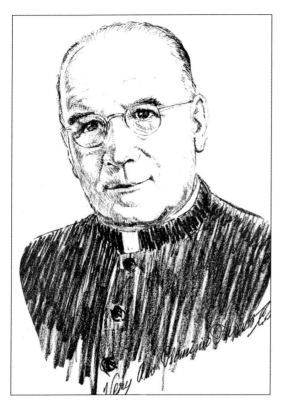

THE VERY REVEREND FLORMINIO
PARENTE, 1967 RECIPIENT. He was
born in Piacenza, Italy, on December
4, 1885. After attending the College of
Missionaries of San Paolo Boromeo, he
was ordained on September 19, 1908.
In 1920, he became acting pastor of
St. Michael's Church in New Haven,
Connecticut, and was later appointed
pastor of St. Bartholomeo's Church in
Providence. In 1922, he became the
pastor of Holy Ghost church, and that
church saw tremendous progress during
his leadership. In 1923, he established
the Holy Ghost Parochial School, and,
in 1939, on the 50th anniversary of
the church, he refinished the entire
interior of the church, in marble, with
artistic murals. In 1936, the King of Italy
decorated Fr. Parente and named him
a Cavaliere. He retired as pastor of the
Holy Ghost Church in 1964. (Courtesy
of Gr "Uff" Joseph R. Muratore
Collection)

GRANDE UFFICALE LUIGI SCALLA, 1968
RECIPIENT, BANKER, CIVIC LEADER, AND
CHAMPION OF ITALIAN CULTURAL ACTIVITIES
IN RHODE ISLAND. Luigi was born in Milazzo,
Sicily, Italy. He came to America in 1910, and
became the Royal Italian consular representative.
In 1924, he became affiliated with the Industrial
Trust Company, and he assisted in the organization
of The Bank of Sicily Trust of New York, of which
he became vice president. In 1934, he became
president of the Columbus National Bank of
Providence, which developed into a leading Italian-
American financial institution in New England.
In 1935, Luigi was elected grand venerable of the
Order Sons of Italy in Rhode Island. He was a
leader in, the study of Italian language, the raising
of funds for the Italian and the American Red
Cross, and many other philanthropic activities. In
1920, the Royal Crown of Italy named honored him
and named him a Cavaliere. In 1930, he married
Marjorie Alford McGuire. (Courtesy of Gr "Uff"
Joseph R. Muratore Collection.)

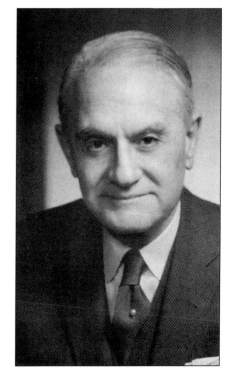

DR. FELIX A. MIRANDO, 1969 RECIPIENT, INDUSTRIALIST, ENTREPRENEUR, AND PHILANTHROPIST. Felix was born in Frosolone, in the province of Campobasso, Italy. He was the co-founder, in 1916, of the Imperial Knife Company. His directorships, of which there are too many to mention, include the Industrial National Bank, Old Colony Cooperative Bank, and Narragansett Electric. In 1955, he was named a Knight of St. Gregory, and then, in 1961, a Knight Commander of St. Gregory. He was also a recipient of the National Brotherhood Award of the National Conference of Christians and Jews. Felix married Auror (DiNoce,) and they were the parents of four children. (Courtesy of Gr "Uff" Joseph R. Muratore Collection.)

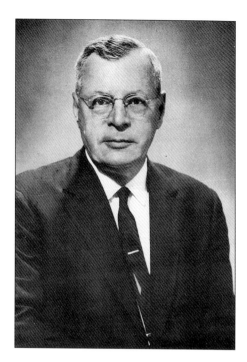

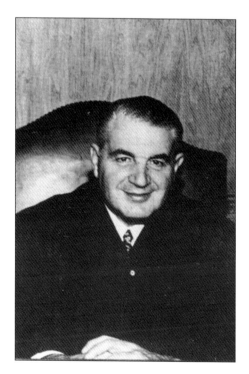

THE HONORABLE CHRISTOPHER DEL SESTO, 1970 RECIPIENT, GOVERNOR, JURIST, AND ADMINISTRATOR. He was born in Providence on March 10, 1907, the son of Eraclio and Rose (Geremia) Del Sesto, who came from Pietravairano, Casserta, Italy. He was a certified public accountant, and an attorney. After graduating Boston University, he attended Georgetown University School of Law. Christopher was state director of price administration, and special assistant to the United States attorney general. He became governor of Rhode Island after serving as associate justice of the Superior Court. As well as being a board member of Johnson & Wales College, Rhode Island School of Design, Providence Public Library, University of Rhode Island, and faculty member of Brown University and northeastern University, he received numerous honorary degrees. He married Lolo F. (Faraone,) and they were the parents of three children, Christopher, Ronald, and Gregory. (Courtesy of Gr "Uff" Joseph R. Muratore Collection.)

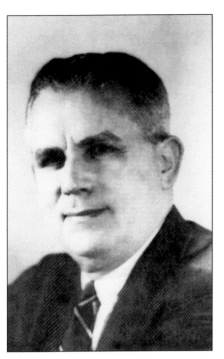

DR. AMERICO A. SAVASTANO, 1971 RECIPIENT, AND OUTSTANDING ORTHOPEDIC SURGEON. Americo was born in Orchi, Italy, on November 28, 1906. He received his education in Providence schools and University of Rhode Island, before attending Harvard University. In 1932, he received his MD degree, and served his residency at the New York Rehabilitation Hospital. He was an instructor in orthopedic surgery at the New York Polyclinic Medical School from 1936 to 1945. In 1959, he was a member of the teaching mission to Israel, and later, during 1963 and 1969, he went to Jordan and Necia. In 1968, he was a member of the Exchange Orthopedic Program to Russia, and he also served as surgeon and chief of orthopedic surgery at the Rhode Island Hospital. In 1967, Americo was team physician at the Pan American Games in Winnipeg, Canada. He married Alda (Winfield,) and they were the parents of two children, Alda Crouchly, and Jeffery W. Savastano. (Courtesy of Gr "Uff" Joseph R. Muratore Collection.)

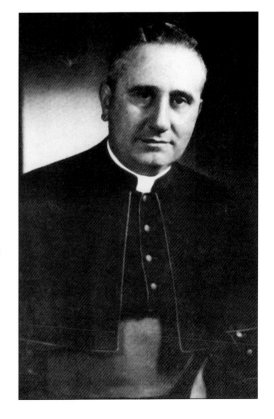

REV. MONSIGNOR ANTHONY L. DIMEO, 1972 RECIPIENT. Monsignor Dimeo was born in Providence, R.I., the son of Luigi and Maria (Zumpetta) Dimeo. He attended St. Ann's Parochial School, and was a member of its first graduating class in 1921. He graduated from Providence College in 1929 and studied at the Pontificio Colletico Leoniano at Hangi, Italy. He was ordained on April 15, 1933, and offered his first mass at St. Ann's Church on September 10, 1933. He arranged for the purchase of the land that St. Rocco's Church is built on. In 1941 he was appointed to the faculty at the Seminary of Our Lady of Providence in Warwick, R.I. In 1952 Monsignor Dimeo was appointed pastor of St. Ann's Parish, becoming the first member of St. Ann's Chruch to become a priest and return to it as its pastor. Two months later he was named a Reverend Monsignor. Courtesy of Gr "Uff" Joseph R. Muratore Collection.)

DR. FIORINDO A. SIMEONE, 1973 RECIPIENT, SURGEON, AND FOUNDER OF THE BROWN UNIVERSITY SCHOOL OF MEDICINE. Born in St. Ambrose, Italy, on January 20, 1908, Fiorindo came to America as a youth, and received his early education in public schools. He attended Brown University, receiving his Master of Science Degree. In 1934, he graduated Harvard Medical School, where he received his M.D. degree, after which he joined the staff of Mass. General. In 1950, he became the director of surgery at the Cleveland Metropolitan General Hospital, and he stayed there until 1967, when he was appointed director of surgery at Miriam Hospital, Providence. In 1967, he became a professor of Medical Science at Brown University. From 1942 to 1946, he was in the Medical Corps of the United States Army, attaining the rank of Colonel. He has received Pro-Tempore appointments in hospitals throughout America, as chief of surgery. He was also a recipient of many other honors that space does not allow to be listed. (Courtesy of Gr "Uff" Joseph R. Muratore Collection.)

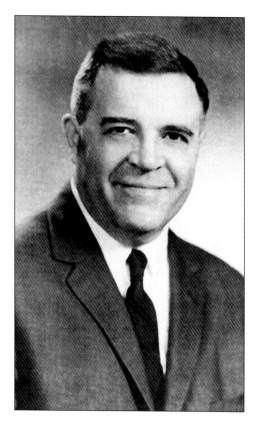

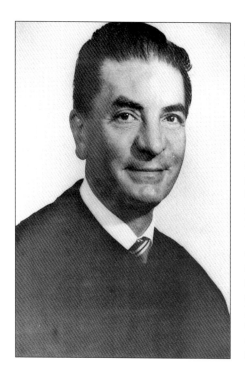

THE HONORABLE RAYMOND J. PETTINE, 1974 RECIPIENT. He was born in Providence, July 6, 1912, the son of James and Aldina (Carulo) Pettine. He attended Providence schools and Providence College, before graduating Boston University School of Law, where he received his LLB and LLM degrees. He served in the United States army during World War II, and returned as a Major and as an active reservist. He retired as Colonel from the Judge Advocate General Corps. On April 19, 1961, Raymond was sworn in as a U.S. attorney for the district of Rhode Island, and was named Chief Judge on May 24, 1971. He rendered many landmark decisions concerning the rights of prisoners. He received many awards, and, in 1967, was named a Knight of St. Gregory. He married Lydia Golini, daughter of Dr. Domenuico Nicola Golini and Dr. Carlotta Nicola (Manente) Golini. Raymond and Lydia were the parents of one daughter, Lydia Pettine. (Courtesy of Gr "Uff" Joseph R. Muratore Collection.)

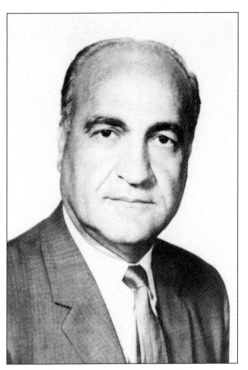

THE HONORABLE JOSEPH A. BEVILACQUA, 1975 RECIPIENT, LEGISLATOR, SPEAKER OF THE HOUSE, AND CHIEF JUDGE OF THE RHODE ISLAND SUPREME COURT. He was born in Providence on December 1, 1918, the son of Giovanni and Angelia (Iannotti) Bevilacqua. After attending Providence public schools, he graduated, in 1940, from Providence College. Joseph was a member of the Rhode Island House of Representatives from 1955 to 1969, when he became Speaker of the House. He was instrumental in establishing the State Medicare Law, and several bills aimed at retraining adults for skilled jobs. He was named Chief Justice for the Rhode Island Supreme Court in 1976. The Italian government honored and named him a Cavalier, to the Order to the Merit of the Republic of Italy. (Courtesy of Gr "Uff" Joseph R. Muratore Collection.)

THE HONORABLE JOHN A. NOTTE JR., 1976 RECIPIENT. Born in Providence, John attended local schools, and graduated from Providence College. He attended Cornell University, and then Boston University Law School, where he received a Jurists Doctorate Degree. In 1943, he enlisted in the United States Navy, served as a gunnery officer, and retired as a lieutenant in 1946. In 1947, he was chairman of the Rhode Island Veterans' Bonus Board, and was appointed to the staff of Senator Theodore Francis Green, serving until 1956. That same year, he was elected secretary of state. Two years later, he was elected lieutenant governor, and, in 1960, he was elected governor of Rhode Island. John was responsible for the creation of the Family Court System. He received honorary degrees from the University of Rhode Island, and was a director of the Roger Williams Law School. In 1975, he was appointed to the Rhode Island Workmen's Compensation Commission by Governor Philip Noel. He was the father of two children, John III, and Joyce. (Couretsy of Gr "Uff" Joseph R. Muratore Collection.)

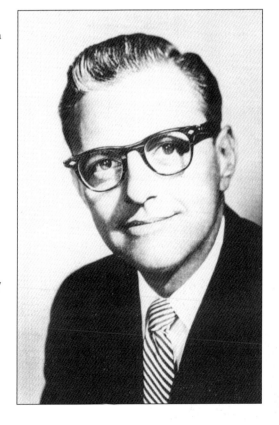

MICHAEL A. GAMMINO JR., 1977 RECIPIENT, BANKER, OUTSTANDING CATHOLIC LAYMAN, AND PHILANTHROPIST. Michael was born in Cranston, RI. He graduated St. Joseph's Academy, Wellesly Hills, Massachusetts, and from Moses Brown School in Providence. In 1947, he graduated Brown University, after which he attended the Graduate School of Philosophy at St. Louis University. In 1969, he was awarded an honorary degree in Humane Letters, by Rhode Island College. He was a veteran of World War II, serving from the shores of Normandy to the Polish border. During the Korean Conflict he was a First Lieutenant in the Air Force Reserve. He became president of Columbus National Bank, and National Columbus Bancorp Inc. As well as being a member of the president's council, of Providence College, he was a member of the board of the Corporation for Public Broadcasting, appointed by President Johnson and President Nixon. In 1978, he was named a Commendatore, by the president of Italy, and in 1977, he was named a Grande "Ufficiale" in The Order to the Merit of the Republic of Italy. He is the father of one daughter. (Courtesy of Gr "Uff" Joseph R. Muratore Collection.)

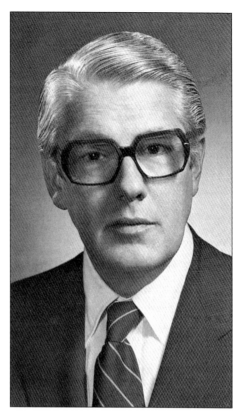

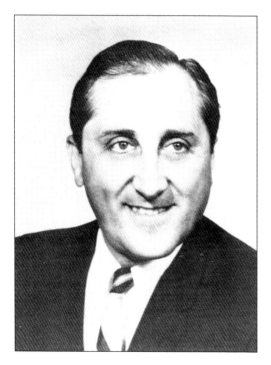

HON. ANTHONY A. GIANNINI, 1978 RECIPIENT, ONE OF THE ABLEST JURISTS SERVING ON THE RHODE ISLAND SUPERIOR COURT. He was born in Providence, R.I., on July 17, 1922, to Antonio and Elvira (Izzi) Giannini. After attending local schools and graduating from LaSalle Academy and Providence College, he attended Boston College Law School, where he received his law degree. He was appointed to the Supreme Court of R.I. in 1951, and was admitted to practice before the Supreme Court of the United States, the United States Court of Appeals for the First Circuit, the United States Court of Military Appeals, and the Federal Court for the District of Rhode Island. He was appointed to the Rhode Island Superior Court in 1969 by Governor Frank Licht. He married Eleanor Ruggierio, and they had four children, Anthony A. Jr., William, Stephen, and Judith. (Courtesy of Gr "Uff" Joseph R. Muratore Collection.)

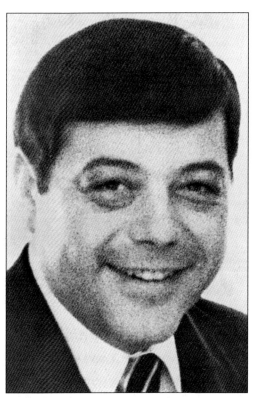

HON. VINCENT ALBERT CIANCI JR., 1979 RECIPIENT, THE YOUNGEST AND FIRST ITALIAN-AMERICAN TO BECOME MAYOR OF PROVIDENCE. Born on April 30, 1941 to Dr. Vincent A. Cianci and Esther (Capobianco) Cianci, Vincent Jr. obtained his elementary and high school education at Moses Brown School in Providence, graduating in 1958. He graduated from Fairfield University in 1962, received his Masters in Political Science from Villanova University Graduate School in 1965, and in 1966 received his Juris Doctor Degree from Marquette University School of Law. While mayor of Providence he became nationally known for his work to revitalize downtown Providence and run-down neighborhoods. He succeeded in bringing a renaissance to the city of Providence. In 1978 he was named a Commendatore by the President of Italy and in 1997 was named a Grande Ufficiale in The Order To The Merit Of The Republic Of Italy. He is the father of one daughter. (Courtesy of Gr "Uff" Joseph R. Muratore Collection.)

CAVALIERE FELIX A. PORCARO, 1980 RECIPIENT, JEWELER, BANKER, AND COMMUNITY LEADER. Felix was born on July 8, 1928, the son of Arthur Porcaro and Margaret (D'Amico) Porcaro. He was educated in Providence schools. He became the founder and president of the Security Back and Trust, Jewels by Felice Inc., Sharon Creations Inc., Jonart Chains Inc., and Treasure of Femic Inc. He was active in many local civic, religious, and fraternal organizations. From 1971 to 1973, he served in the Rhode Island General Assembly as representative. In 1978, he was awarded the Italian Star of Solidarity, and named a Cavaliere, in the Order to the Merit of the Republic of Italy. He married Marie Porcaro, and they were the parents of five children, Linda Cerise, Beverly Casinelli, Flex A. Jr., Patrick, and Vincent. (Courtesy of Gr "Uff" Joseph R. Muratore Collection.)

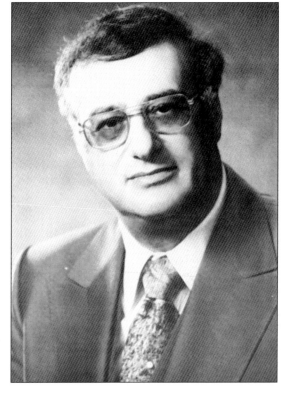

REV. MSGR. GALLIANO J. CAVALLARO, 1981
RECIPIENT, CHURCH LEADER, AND OUTSTANDING
CIVIC LEADER. Rev. Msgr. was born in Providence,
November 9, 1914, the son of Giuseppe and
Angelina (Tomasso) Cavallaro. He graduated La
Salle Academy, and attended St. Charles College
at Catonsville, Maryland, graduating in 1937. He
attended St. Mary's Seminar, Baltimore, and was
ordained on December 19, 1942, in his home parish,
Our Lady of Mount Carmel Church. In 1959, he was
appointed director of Catholic Cemeteries for the
diocese of Providence. In 1995, he was appointed
diocesan chaplain for Italian immigrants, and of
Italian-speaking civic religious societies. During his
pastorship of Our Lady of Mount Carmel Church, he
completely renovated the interior of the church, and
purchased, with church funds, the land and buildings
surrounding it, developing the land into a park-like
area. He spearheaded the renaissance of Federal
Hill. In 1979, a granite bust and shaft was erected in
his honor at the corner of Dean Street and Atwells
Avenue, Providence. He retired in 1990 as pastor,
though he continued as Director of Cemeteries. He
still leads a full schedule, offering Masses throughout
the state. (Courtesy of Gr "Uff" Joseph R. Muratore
Collection.)

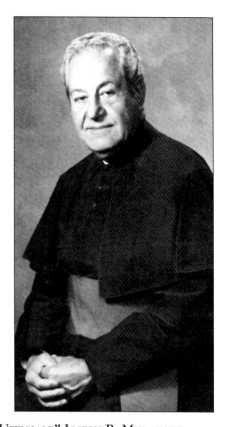

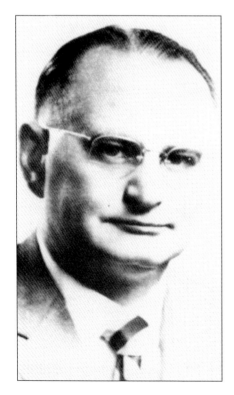

GRANDE "UFFICIALE" JOSEPH R. MURATORE,
1982 RECIPIENT, ITALIAN VICE CONSUL (RET.)
Joseph was born in Providence, August 8, 1921,
the son of Sebastian and Lena (Curione) Muratore.
He graduated from Central High School in June
of 1939, entered the U.S. Army in October 1942,
and was honorably discharged in December
1945. Joseph was the founder and president of
Muratore Agency Inc., Muratore Realty Corp.,
Columbus Mortgage & Loan Corp. of Rhode Island,
Shawomet Holding Associates, Chariho Investors,
Federal Hill Associates, and many other investment
corporations. He was decorated by the Dominican
Republic in 1969 as a Commendatore and a Grande
Ufficiale. In 1974, he was decorated by the Italian
government as a Cavaliere Ufficiale, and, in 1977,
Commedatore. He was also awarded the Italian
Star in the rank of Grande Ufficiale, all in the
Order to the Merit of the Republic of Italy. He is a
contributing author to numerous periodicals, and is
the author of this work. In 1943, he married Rose E.
(DiMeglio) Muratore, and they were the parents of
two children, Joseph R. Jr., a Warwick attorney, and
Joy A. Malone, a New York attorney. (Courtesy of
Gr "Uff" Joseph R. Muratore Collection.)

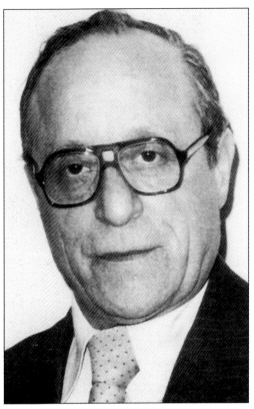

REPRESENTATIVE ALDO FREDA, 1983 RECIPIENT, VETERAN LEGISLATOR, RECOGNIZED COMMUNITY LEADER, DEDICATED PUBLIC SERVANT, CONCERNED HUMANITARIAN, AND PROMOTER OF ITALIAN CULTURE AND HERITAGE. He was born on July 18, 1921, and he attended Providence schools, graduating Central High School. He was district office supervisor for John Hancock Life Insurance Company, and from 1942 to 1946, he served as sergeant in the radar section of the U.S. Army. In 1960, he was elected to the Rhode Island House of Representatives, serving from Providence's 14th District for twelve, two-year terms, longer than any other state senator or representative. He was Dean of Legislators in the General Assemble, Deputy Majority Leader from 1969 through 1977, and Speaker Pro Tempore from 1977 to 1980. For many years, he sponsored summer picnics and Christmas parties, which were attended by thousands. The proceeds were used to benefit under-privileged children of Federal Hill. He was unmarried. (Courtesy of Gr "Uff" Joseph R. Muratore Collection.)

THE HONORABLE SALVATORE MANCINI, 1984 RECIPIENT, VETERAN CIVIC, AND CHARITABLE ORGANIZATION LEADER. He was born in Cranston, the son of Mr. and Mrs. Vincent Mancini, and attended school in the Knighsville section of Cranston, graduating Cranston High School. Salvatore was a veteran of World War II, and after military service, he joined his brother's electrical business and founded the Ace Hardware Store in Centerdale. The store was operated by Salvatore until he was elected, in 1973, to be North Providence's first mayor. He was president of Sal Mancini Associates Inc., Oakwood Homes Inc., and Professional Development Inc. In support of the advancement of Italian culture, he served as a member of the American-Italian Cultural Exchange Commission, the Italian-American Club, Aurora Civic Association, and the Scalabrini Villa Development Campaign. (Courtesy of Gr "Uff" Joseph R. Muratore Collection.)

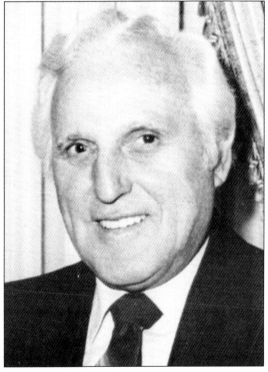

CONRAD FERLA, 1986 RECIPIENT, AND PRESIDENT OF ROCKY POINT PARK. Conrad was born in Syracuse, Sicily, in 1921. He moved, with his family, to Northern Africa when he was 10 years old. In 1941, he was drafted into the Italian Army, serving until he was captured in Tunisia in 1943. In 1949, he came to Rhode Island to join his brother Vincent, who owned Rocky Point Park. Starting as a handyman, he worked up to be president and general manager, becoming known as "Mr. Rocky Point." Although extremely busy at Rocky Point Park, he was very active in civic, fraternal, and charitable organizations. He served as president of Big Brother of Rhode Island, Warwick Businessmen's Association, and so many other civic and charitable organizations that space does not allow their listing. For his services to the Italian-American community, Conrad was decorated by the Italian government, in the Order to the Merit of the Republic of Italy, and was named a Cavaliere in 1992. He married Anita (Cerri) Ferla, and they were the parents of Alan Robert and Conrad Jr. (Courtesy of Gr "Uff" Joseph R. Muratore Collection.)

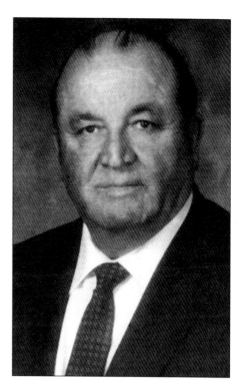

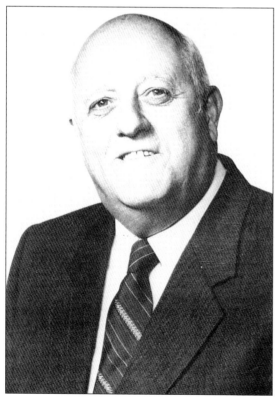

SERAFINO G. LONARDO JR., 1986 RECIPIENT. Serafino Jr., a humble, unassuming quiet man who influenced the lives of many in a positive way, was born in Providence, R.I., one of 14 children of Serafino and Palmarosa Lonardo, who were Italian immigrants. Serafina Jr. would like best to be described as a man who lives close to nature, which is evident in his love of gardening. Joe, as he is known to his friends, has been active in church affairs, and has ben a trustee of his church for many years. For 11 years he worked as a volunteer raising funds for the Arthur Trudeau Center. he was co-founder of the DaVinci Center for Community Progress, Inc. and served as its president for 10 years. In 1946 he began working in the jewelry business and became plant manager of the Imperial Pearl Company. He married the former Elena (Valente) Testa, and they live in Providence. (Courtesy of Gr "Uff" Joseph R. Muratore Collection.)

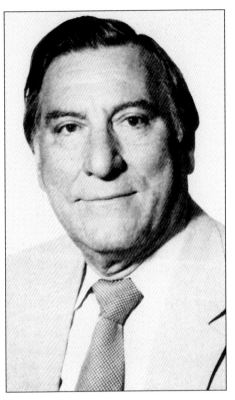

JOSEPH TERINO, 1987 RECIPIENT. Joseph was born in Providence, 1916, the son of Pasquale, who was born in Teano, Italy in 1890. His mother Pasqualina (DeGuillo) Terino was born in Naples in 1900. He established Tercat Tool & Die Company in 1936, when only 20 years old, in a garage at 82 Cedar Street, later building a modern building at 31 Delaine Street, Providence. He has been engaged in the jewelry stamping business, which has involved the stamping of cosmetic, pet, industrial, commercial coining, and premium articles, in all types of metals. He has been an active member of civic, fraternal, and charitable organizations, among them, the North Providence Boys and Girls Clubs, Italio-American Club, Scalabrini Villa, Bishop's Council of St. Joseph, Jewelers Board of Trades, and member of the North Providence Zoning Board. For his services to the Italian-American community in Rhode Island, he was named a Cavaliere, in the Order to the Merit of the Republic of Italy. In 1940, he married Palmina A. (D'Martino) Terino. They were the parents of three children, Joyce Procaccini, Joseph Jr., and Robert.(Courtesy of Gr "Uff" Joseph R. Muratore Collection.)

JOSEPH A. ALMAGNO, 1988 RECIPIENT, SUPERINTENDENT OF PROVIDENCE PUBLIC SCHOOLS. He was born in Providence on October 19, 1941, the son of Stephen and Theresa (LaFazia) Almagno. He was educated in Providence public schools, and graduated Lasalle Academy. Siena College, New York, was where he received his BA degree in 1964, and he went on to earn his masters degree, in 1971, from Providence College. Joseph has been an educator for more than 25 years, rising from schoolteacher to superintendent. After teaching for eight years, he was appointed principal of Webster Avenue and Academy Avenue Schools, also serving as compensatory education administrator, and deputy assistant superintendent for Curriculum and Instruction. He was elected on March 9, 1987, as superintendent of schools, by a unanimous vote of the Providence School Board, and was responsible for over 20,000 students and 2,000 employees in 31 schools. He married Marie (Mansolillo) Almagno, a registered nurse, and they became the parents of two children, Stephanie and Stephen. (Courtesy of Gr "Uff" Joseph R. Muratore Collection.)

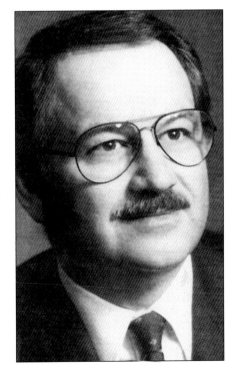

GOVERNOR EDWARD D. DiPRETE, 1989 RECIPIENT. He was born in Cranston on July 8, 1934, and was a graduate of LaSalle Academy and Holy Cross College. He received honorary degrees from Holy Cross College, Bryant College, Providence College, University of Rhode Island, and many other colleges. He is a veteran of the U.S. Navy, and the Naval Reserves, where he held the rank of Lt. Commander. He was elected to his third term as governor of Rhode Island on November 8, 1988. He served as mayor of Cranston, first being elected in 1978, and then re-elected in 1982, with 83 percent of the vote, the largest plurality in the history of Cranston. He was a city councilman from 1974 to 1978, and a school committee member from 1970 to 1974. Among the programs he implemented, while Governor, are, the Education Improvement Act of 1988, the Literacy and Dropout Prevention Act of 1987, and a multi-million dollar Excellence in Education Fund. He married Patricia (Hines) DiPrete, and they are the parents of seven children. (Courtesy of Gr "Uff" Joseph R. Muratore Collection.)

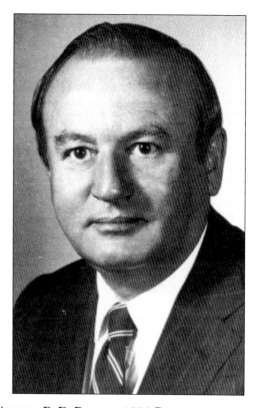

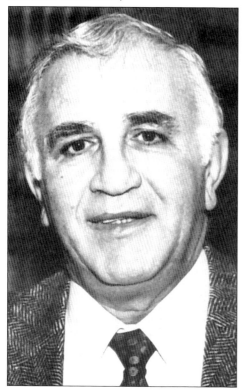

ALBERT E. DeROBBIO, 1990 RECIPIENT, CHIEF JUDGE OF RHODE ISLAND DISTRICT COURT. He was born in Providence on July 13, 1929, the son of Ernest O. DeRobbio and Maria (Della Grotta) DeRobbio, who came to America from Italy. He attended Providence schools, graduated Boston College in 1951, and received his law degree from Boston University Law School in 1956. He served in the U.S. Army from 1951 to 1953. In 1967, he joined the staff of the Attorney General's office, and served as Assistant Attorney General in various capacities, and as a Chief of the Criminal Division. In 1976, he was appointed an Associate Justice of the District Court. In 1979, Governor J. Joseph Garrahy appointed him Associate Justice of the Superior Court, and in 1987, he was appointed Chief Judge of the Rhode Island District Court. He has served on numerous commissions and committees of the Judiciary. He has also been an active community leader, serving on many boards. He is married to Barbara M. (Ardizzone) DeRobbio. They are the parents of five children. (Courtesy of Gr "Uff" Joseph R. Muratore Collection.)

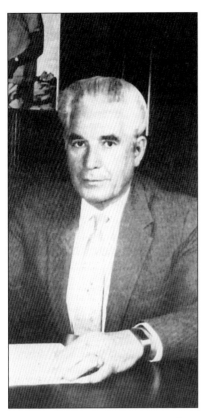

RALPH R. A'RUSSO, 1991 RECIPIENT, AND MAYOR OF JOHNSTON, RI. Ralph was born in Johnston on April 25, 1924, the son of Domenico and Maria (Ricci) Russo. He attended Johnston schools, and graduated from Central High School. He joined the U.S. Marine Corps in 1942, and attended Grove City College, PA, before becoming Communications Chief, at Corpus Christi, Texas. He spent 18 months in the Asiatic Theatre of Operations in the Marshall Islands, and participated in the invasion of Okinawa. He later served in Japan with the occupational forces, and was one of the first marines sent to Japan. He saw the destruction of Hiroschima, the scene of the first atom bombing. He was discharged in 1946. Ralph attended Bryant College and Johnson & Wales for the study of business law, banking, financing, and human relations. In 1960, he was elected to the Johnston town council, and served as its first finance director. In 1970, he was elected mayor, a position that he held for 20 years. Ralph was active in many civic, religious, and fraternal organizations, including the Kelley Gazzero VFW Post, the American Legion Post '94, the Zoning Board of Review, the Order Sons of Italy, Loggia Pontecorvo, and many others. He married Tina (Butera) Russo, and they are the parents of five children. (Courtesy of Gr "Uff" Joseph R. Muratore Collection.)

LINDA D'AMARIO ROSSI, 1992 RECIPIENT, DIRECTOR OF RHODE ISLAND DEPARTMENT OF CHILDREN, YOUTH AND FAMILIES. Linda is the daughter of Mr. and Mrs. Amedeo D'Amario of Cranston. She received a Bachelor of Science degree in child development, from University of Rhode Island, in 1968, followed by her masters from Boston University School of Social Work, in 1974. She studied strategic management at the University of Pennsylvania, Wharton School, in 1978, and attended Harvard University's John F. Kennedy School of Government in 1990. From 1974 to 1976, she was coordinator of the residential services unit in the Rhode Island Department of Corrections. Between 1983 and 1985, she was director of the Rhode Island Department of Children, Youth and Families. She was appointed deputy commissioner of the Texas Youth Commission between 1985 and 1987, and from 1987 to 1991 she became secretary to the Maryland Department of Juvenile Services in Baltimore, Maryland. In 1991, Linda returned to Rhode Island as director of the Rhode Island Department of Children, Youth and Families. She has received many professional honors, including the Creative Public Administration Award in 1977, and in 1988, she received the E.R. Case Correctional Achievement Award, the highest award given by the American Correctional Association. She was married to Judge Angelo G. Rossi, who is deceased. (Courtesy of Gr "Uff" Joseph R. Muratore Collection.)

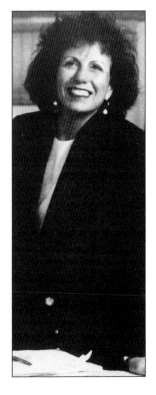

CHIEF VINCENT A. VESPIA, 1993 RECIPIENT, CHIEF OF POLICE, SOUTH KINGSTON. He was born in Providence, the eldest of three sons, to Vincent and Eileen Vespia. He attended local schools, graduating Hope High School in 1956, before serving in the U.S. Army until he was honorably discharged in 1958. His professional training and education started when he graduated from the Rhode Island State Police Academy in 1959, and was appointed a member of Rhode Island State Police. He attended the Federal Bureau of Narcotics Training School in 1967, and the New England State Police Administration Conference Organized Crime School in 1969. In 1969, he was promoted to Detective Corporal, and in 1972, was assigned acting Chief of Police of Coventry. On completion of that assignment, he was offered to remain permanently as Coventry's Police Chief, but he chose to return to the State Police, investigating organized crime. In 1978, he was promoted to Detective Lieutenant, and became the principal investigator of the organized crime unit. After 22 years as a state police officer, he became Police Chief of South Kingstown, in 1981. He has received many honors and recognitions, and has been featured in national publications. His commendations are many, and space does not allow for their listing. He is married to Judith-Ann Vespia, and they are the parents of three daughters, Rhonda, Renee, and Robin. (Courtesy of Gr "Uff" Joseph R. Muratore Collection.)

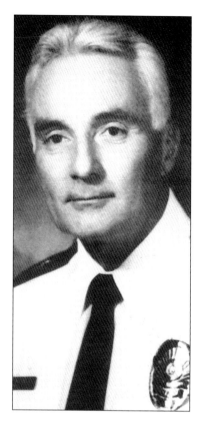

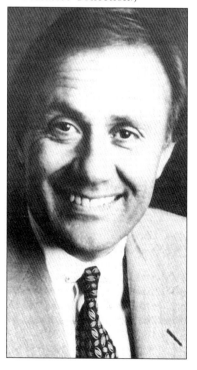

ARTHUR A. COIA, 1994 RECIPIENT, GENERAL PRESIDENT OF THE LABORERS' INTERNATIONAL UNION OF NORTH AMERICA, SKILLED ATTORNEY, ASTUTE NEGOTIATOR, PERSUASIVE ORGANIZER, AND A POWERFUL ORATOR. Since 1993, Arthur has been general president of the Laborers' International Union of North America (LIUNA,) one of the largest and most diverse unions in the AFL-CIO. A Providence native, Arthur joined LIUNA as a teenager, while working his way through Providence College and Boston University Law School. He has been admitted to practice law before the U.S. Supreme Court. He has been an officer of AFL-CIO Executive Council, a member of the Blue Ribbon Committee on health care reform, and on governing boards of presidents of the AFL-CIO Building and Construction Trades Department. He is also a trustee of the AFL-CIO Housing Investment Trust, co-chairman of the Laborers' National Pension Fund and Laborers National (Industrial) Pension Fund, and chairman of theLaborers' Political League (LPL.) He married Joanne (Ciaccia) Coia in 1967, and they are the parents of two children, Christen and Arthur, and the grandparents of two. (Courtesy of Gr "Uff" Joseph R. Muratore Collection.)

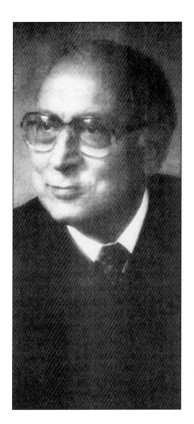

THE HONORABLE VINCENT A. RAGOSTA, 1995 RECIPIENT, ASSOCIATE JUSTICE OF RHODE ISLAND SUPERIOR COURT. He was born in Providence on February 12, 1924, the son of Domenico and Rose (Bottis) Ragosta. He attended Providence public schools, and the University of Rhode Island in 1942. World War II interrupted his education; he served in the armed forces from 1943 to 1946 with overseas duty in the Pacific Theater. Resuming his studies at the University of Rhode Island, he graduated in 1949, receiving his Bachelor of Science degree, before entering Boston College Law School, where he received his Juris Doctor degree in 1951. He also attended John Hopkins University and The Citadel. He is a member of the American Trial Lawyers Association and many other professional, civic, fraternal, and religious organizations. He has been an active member of the Order Sons of Italy (achieving the highest office of Grand Venerable in 1971), a National Trustee of the Supreme Lodge of the Order, and a member of the Verrazzano Day Observance Committee Inc. In 1975, he was honored by the Italian government, receiving the title of Cavaliere, in the Order to the Merit of the Republic of Italy. He is married to Carmela (Bruno) Ragosta, and they are the parents of four sons, Vincent Jr. Esq.; Dominic L., CPA; and Peter J. Sr., RPH. (Courtesy of Gr "Uff" Joseph R. Muratore Collection.)

AMBASSADOR JOSEPH R. PAOLINO JR., 1996 RECIPIENT. He was born in Providence on April 26, 1955, the son of Joseph R. Paolino and Beatrice (DePasquale) Temkin, the grandson of the late Judge and Mrs. Luigi DePasquale, and the grandnephew of the late Rhode Island Supreme Court Justice Thomas J. Paolino. He graduated from LaSalle Academy, and from Roger Williams University in 1978, receiving a Bachelor of Science Degree, before earning a Master of Liberal Arts degree in Government from the Harvard University Extension School in 1989. His appointment to the Providence Historic District Commission in 1974 began his political career. In 1977, he became Administrative Assistant to the Lieutenant Governor, and in 1978, he was elected councilman for the Federal Hill section. In 1983, he was elected council president, and he served as mayor of the city of Providence from 1984 to 1991. Thereafter, Joseph was appointed by the governor to serve as director of the Department of Economic Development, until President Clinton named him as U.S. Ambassador to the Republic of Malta. He was instrumental in bringing national companies to located their headquarters at the old train station, which was restored through his efforts. He is married to Lianne (Andreoni) Paolino, and they are the parents of four children, Jennifer, Christina, Jacqueline, and Joseph III. (Courtesy of Gr "Uff" Joseph R. Muratore Collection.)

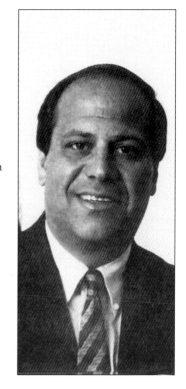

THE HONORABLE EVELYN V. FARGNOLI, 1997
RECIPIENT, PRESIDENT OF PROVIDENCE CITY
COUNCIL. Evelyn was born in Providence on
November 5, 1923, the daughter of Antonio and
Bernadine (Verdi). She attended Providence public
schools, graduating from Central High School in
January of 1941. Her political career began in 1981
after the death of her husband, Ralph R. Fargnoli,
when she was elected to fill his unexpired term. She
was subsequently re-elected in 1982, 1986, 1990,
and 1994. She served on the Finance Committee,
Claims Committee, and Water Supervisory Board,
and became chairperson of these bodies. She was
elected president of the city council on June 20,
1996. She owns and operates the Specialty Cleaners
in the Mount Pleasant section of Providence, and is
a member of the Rhode Island College Foundation,
the Providence College President's Council, and
many other civic organizations. Evelyn and her late
husband, Ralph R. Fargnoli, were the parents of two
children, Mary-Ellen Fargnoli, of New Jersey, and
John A. Fargnoli, of Providence. (Courtesy of Gr
"Uff" Joseph R. Muratore Collection.)

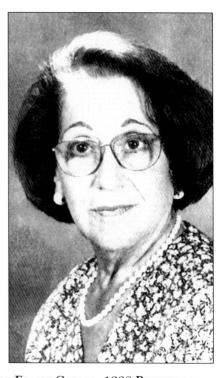

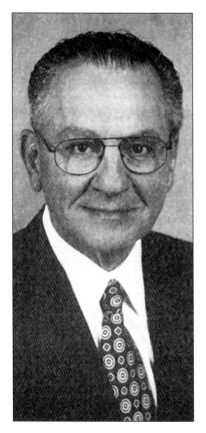

THE HONORABLE FRANK CAPRIO, 1998 RECIPIENT,
CHIEF JUDGE OF PROVIDENCE MUNICIPAL COURT. He
was born in Providence on November 24, 1936, the son
of immigrant parents. He attended Providence public
schools, graduating in 1958 from Providence College
with a Bachelor of Arts degree. He earned an Education
Certificate from Rhode Island College in 1959. While
teaching at Hope High School, he attended Suffolk
University Law School in the evenings, and received his
Juris Doctor degree in 1965. In 1985, he was appointed
a Providence Municipal Court Judge, becoming its
chief judge in 1990. He became a well-known public
figure, after appearing regularly on television, where
he distinguished himself for his sound judgment,
compassionate justice, and quick wit. He is the senior
partner in the Caprio & Caprio Law Firm. His public
service began in 1962, when he was elected to the
Providence City Council, representing Federal Hill,
and serving on the city council for eight years. Frank
is a member of the Rhode Island Board of Governors
for Higher Education, and a member of many civic,
fraternal, charitable, and religious organizations. As
a successful businessman, he is principal owner of the
Coast Guard House, Casey's Restaurant, and Cherry Hill
Housing in Johnston. He married Joyce (Tibaldi), and
they are the parents of five children, Frank T., David A.,
Marissa, John, and Paul. (Courtesy of Gr "Uff" Joseph R.
Muratore Collection.)

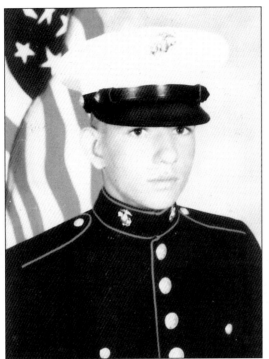

CORPORAL EDWARD S. IACOVINO JR.
He was one of 229 marines who died on October 23, 1983, when a truck loaded with explosives was driven into the compound of the Marine Peacekeeping Force in Beirut, Lebanon. That massacre was described by Col. Donald R. Gardiner, director of the 1st Marine District, as the nation's greatest single day of casualties in a combat-related situation since World War II. Edward was the son of Elizabeth and Edward Iacovino Sr. (Courtesy of Gr "Uff" Joseph R. Muratore Collection.)

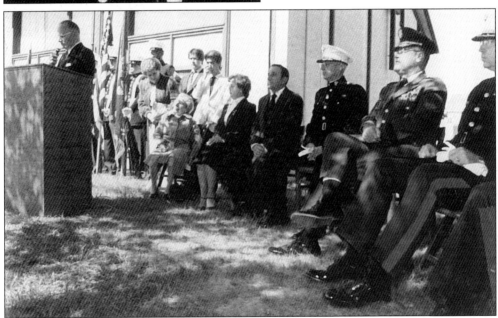

COMM. JOSEPH R. MURATORE ADDRESSING AN AUDIENCE AT IACOVINO SQUARE, SEPTEMBER 16, 1984. This speech, delivered at the corner of Beach Avenue and West Shore Road, Warwick, was dedicated in memory of Cpl. Edward S. Iacovino Jr., a 20-year old serviceman, who was killed in the terrorist bombing of Marine headquarters in Beirut, Lebanon. This dedication was attended by over 600 people. Included in this photograph are Mr. and Mrs. Edward Iacovino Sr., various Marine Corp Generals, Police Chief John Coutcher, and Mayor Charles Donovan. (Courtesy of Gr "Uff" Joseph R. Muratore Collection.)

THE VILLAGE OF CONIMICUT, WARWICK, HONORING CPL. IACOVINO, ONE OF ITS FALLEN SONS. At this dedication ceremony were approximately 600 people, many of who were Cpl. Iacovino's family and friends. There were also contingents from the William Shields Post, American Legion 43; VFW Post 272; VFW Post 183; and the West Shore Imperial Band. Pictured, from left to right are, Mrs. Elizabeth Iacovino, Edward Iacovino Sr., and Comm. Joseph R. Muratore. This village has given, the state of Rhode Island, a governor; the city, two mayors; the United States, a major general; and now, a son in a mission of peace. The dedication ceremony was held following a Mass that was celebrated at St. Benedicts Church. Leading the group included, the West Shore Imperials Drum & Bugle Corps, the Ocean State Band, and the Warwick Police Color Guard. In solemn procession, those who attended arrived at the four corners of Beach Avenue and West Shore Road, where the dedication ceremonies were held. Participating in the ceremonies were Col. Gardiner; Gen. John J. Salesses, past commanding general of the 4th Marine Division; and Councilman Walter Santos. (Courtesy of Gr "Uff" Joseph R. Muratore Collection.)

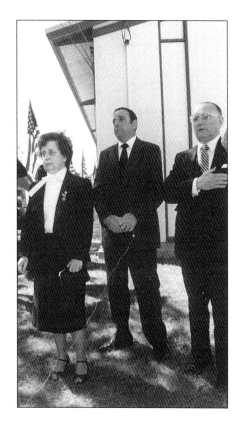

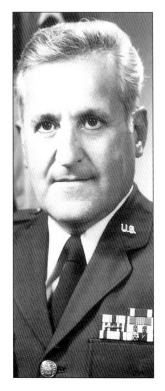

BRIGADEER GENERAL NICHOLAS ANNICELLI JR. (RET.) He is the former assistant general and deputy commanding general for Air, Rhode Island Air National Guard, and the commanding general, Rhode Island National Guard from 1984 to 1988. He was born September 13, 1929, in the Federal Hill section of Providence. He is the son of Cora (Calise) and Nicholas Annicelli, who were born in Ischia, Naples, Italy. After graduating Mount Pleasant High School in 1947, he received his Bachelor of Science degree in business administration from Bryant College, Providence, in 1950. He attended the U.S. Air Force Information Service Officer Course, Maxwell Air Force Base, Ala. in 1958; Squadron Officer's School, Maxwell Air Base, Ala. in 1959; Air Command and Staff College, in 1970; and Air War College, in 1972. Following his entry to the U.S. Air Force in 1948, he was released from active duty as a sergeant and reassigned to the Enlisted Reserve Corps. In 1949, he joined the 152nd Fighter Squadron, RI Air National Guard, and served continuously until his retirement. In 1956, he received a direct commission as 2nd Lieutenant. He received eight decorations and awards, and several Rhode Island National Guard Awards. In 1985, he was promoted to brigadier general. He retired from the Air National Guard on August 6, 1988. He is married to Rosemarie (Marandola), and they are the parents of two daughters, Patricia A., and Judy L. (Courtesy of Gr "Uff" Joseph R. Muratore Collection.)

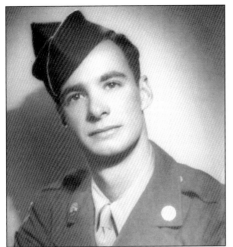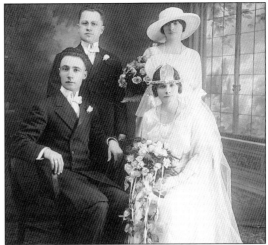

LEFT: CORPORAL S. JOSEPH MANDATO. He attended Central High School, Bryant College, and the Williams School of Banking, where he received a degree in Business Administration. He retired from Fleet National, where he had served as manager in various branches. During World War II, he served in China, in part of the Burma India Theatre of Operations, and was engaged in three battles, receiving three battle stars for this action. He was captured, and was one of the prisoners in the forced Burma March, in which hundreds of American soldiers died. His father, Vincenzo Mandato, was born in 1893 in Caserta, Italy, and he came to the United States in 1912. He was a silk weaver. His mother was Rosina (DePasquale) Mandato, who was born in 1895 in Compobasso, Italy. His hobby is to decorate War Veterans' graves with American Flags. He married Asunta Nardi in 1953. RIGHT: VINCENZO AND ROSINA (DEPASQUALE) MANDATO, PARENTS OF JOSEPH MANDATO. Their maid of honor was Angelia DePasquale, sister of the bride, cousin of Judge Luigi DePasquale. Judge DePasquale became a family friend while attending school, and their friendship endured throughout their lifetime. (Courtesy of Gr "Uff" Joseph R. Muratore Collection.)

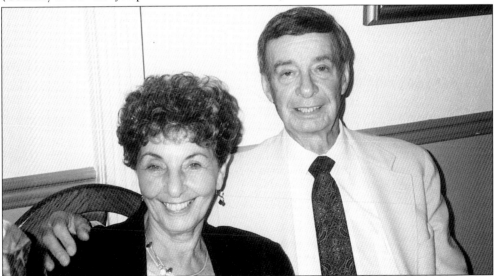

JOSEPH MANDATO AND ASUNTA (SUE) MANDATO ON THEIR 45TH WEDDING ANNIVERSARY, APRIL 25, 1988. They are the parents of one son, Joseph. (Courtesy of Gr "Uff" Joseph R. Muratore Collection.)

Six

ITALIAN AMERICANS IN THE CREATION OF R.I.

The Italians and the Creation of America is a book that was published by the John Carter Brown Library. The library contains some of the most valuable and original maps, documents and reference books, as part of the excellent collection at Brown University, Providence. The publishing of *The Italians and the Creation of America* resulted in a display of rare books, documents, and original maps at the John Carter Brown Library. The exhibit was attended by the Ambassador of Italy, Roberto Gaja, the consul general of Italy for New England, Franco Faa' di Bruno, and many other notable Rhode Islanders, including mayors, the governor, members of the judiciary, and representatives from all walks of life. This display was later exhibited at the Smithsonian Institute, Washington, D.C., and followed by a private reception at the ambassador's residence. Later, this collection was also exhibited in Florence, Italy. The members of this special committee were, Cav. Vincent J. Buonanno, chairman; Samuel Hough, assistant librarian, John

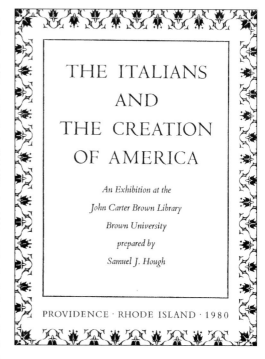

THE ITALIANS

AND

THE CREATION

OF AMERICA

An Exhibition at the

John Carter Brown Library

Brown University

prepared by

Samuel J. Hough

PROVIDENCE · RHODE ISLAND · 1980

Carter Brown Library; Ronald W. Del Sesto; Albert E. Carlotti; Michael A. Gammino; Comm. Joseph R. Muratore; Judge Thomas J. Paolino; Dr. Fiorindo A. Simeone; Mr. Temple Smith; Mr. James Twaddell; Dr. Armand B. Versaci; and the executive committee of the associates of the John Carter Brown Library. They raised funds through a private solicitation, to make the printing of this book possible. (Courtesy of Gr "Uff" Joseph R. Muratore Collection.)

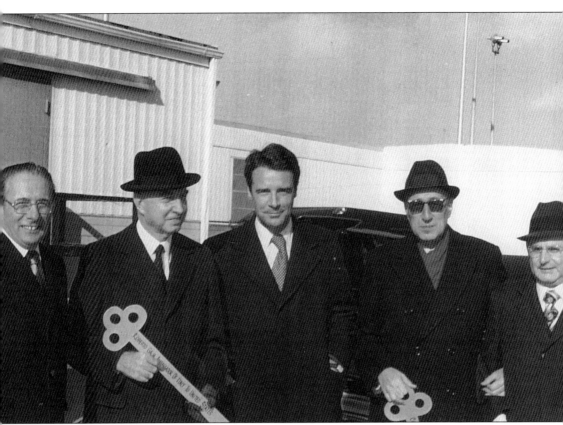

ON THE OCCASION OF THE DISPLAY OF RARE ITALIAN DOCUMENTS AND MAPS, AT THE JOHN CARTER BROWN LIBRARY, DECEMBER 9, 1976, Pictured, from left to right, are, William Leonelli, Warwick city treasurer; Roberto Gaja, Italy's ambassador to the United States; Vincent Buonanno Jr.; Dr. Franco Faa' Di Bruno, Italian consul general in Boston for New England; and Comm. Joseph R. Muratore, Italian vice council (Ret.) for Rhode Island. They are greeting Ambassador Gaja and Consul General Faa' di Bruno, who both arrived in Rhode Island for this event at Brown University. (Courtesy of Gr "Uff" Joseph R. Muratore Collection.)

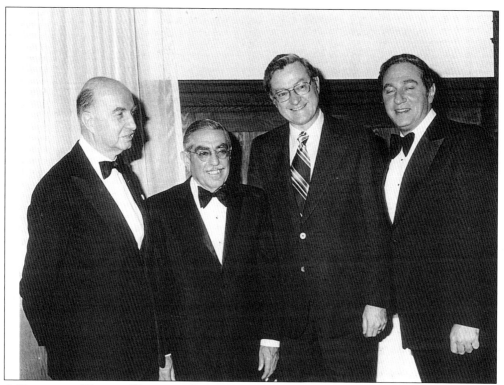

A Reception Held in Honor of Roberto Gaya, Ambassador of Italy to the United States. This event was held at the Hope Club, in Providence. In the above picture, from left to right, are Ambassador Roberto Gaja, Senator John O. Pastore, Governor J. Joseph Garraghy, and Lt. Gov. Thomas DiLuglio. In the photograph below, from left to right, are Ambassador Roberto Gaja, Mrs. Gaja, Cav. Vincent Buonanno Jr., and Mrs. Nicholas Brown. They are enjoying roaming musicians, who were led by Dr. Joseph Conti. (Both images courtesy of Gr "Uff" Joseph R. Muratore Collection.)

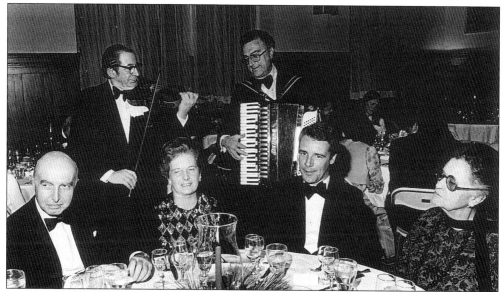

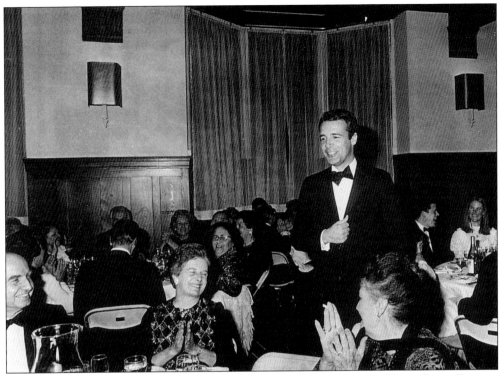

CAV. VINCENT BUANANNO JR., ADDRESSING DINNER GUESTS AT THE HOPE CLUB, BROWN UNIVERSITY. The occasion was a reception, held in honor of Ambassador Roberto Gaja, Ambassador of Italy to the United States. Pictured here, from left to right, are Amb. Gaja, Mrs. Gaja, and Cav. Vincent Buonanno Jr. Behind Mrs. Gaja is Mrs. Raymond J. Pettine. (Courtesy of Gr "Uff" Joseph R. Muratore Collection.)

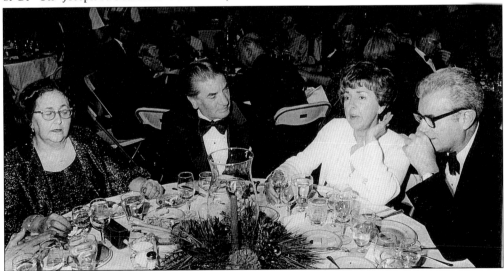

SOME OF THE GUESTS AT THE RECEPTION IN HONOR OF AMBASSADOR ROBERTO GAJA. Shown, from left to right, are, Mrs. Raymond J. Pettine; Hon. Raymond J. Pettine, chief judge of Rhode Island Federal Court; Mrs. Gloria Lancelotti; and Dante Lancelotti. (Courtesy of Gr "Uff" Joseph R. Muratore Collection.)

110

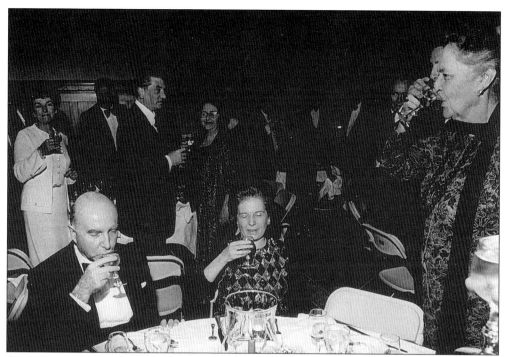

ACKNOWLEDGING A TOAST AT THE RECEPTION IN HONOR OF AMBASSADOR ROBERTO GAJA. Pictured, from left to right, are, (seated) Amb. Gaja; Mrs. Gaja; and Mrs. John Nicholas Brown; (standing) Mrs. Gloria Lancelotti; Hon. Raymond J. Pettine, chief judge of Rhode Island Federal Court; and Mrs. Pettine. (Courtesy of Gr "Uff" Joseph R. Muratore Collection.)

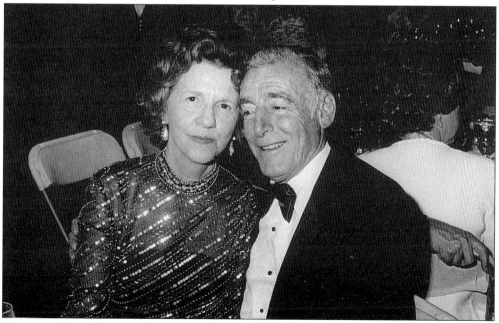

MR. AND MRS. VINCENT BUONANNO SR. AT THE RECEPTION IN HONOR OF AMBASSADOR ROBERTO GAJA AT THE HOPE CLUB, BROWN UNIVERSITY. (Courtesy of Gr "Uff" Joseph R. Muratore Collection.)

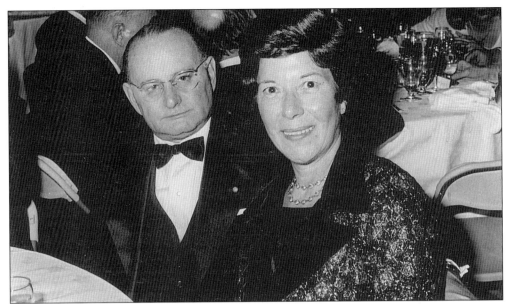

COMM. JOSEPH R. MURATORE AND MRS. JOSEPH R. MURATORE, GUESTS AT THE RECEPTION IN HONOR OF AMBASSADOR ROBERTO GAJA. (Courtesy of Gr "Uff" Joseph R. Muratore Collection.)

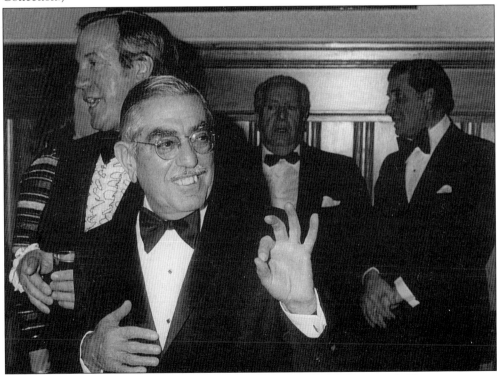

SENATOR JOHN O. PASTORE, EXPRESSING APPROVAL OF THE EVENING'S EVENTS AT THE RECEPTION FOR AMBASSADOR ROBERTO GAJA. Pictured, from left to right, are, David Zucconni, special events director at Brown University; Sen. Umberto Patalano; and Chief Judge Raymond J. Pettine. (Courtesy of Gr "Uff" Joseph R. Muratore Collection.)

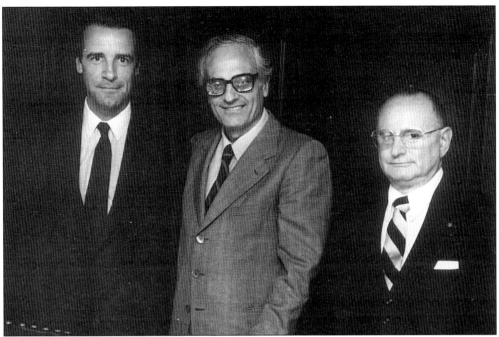

A 1979 RECEPTION HELD FOR VINCENT J. BUONANNO JR. IN BOSTON. This occasion followed Vincent's decoration, by the Italian government, as Cavaliere, to the Merit of the Order to the Republic of Italy. He was named in recognition of his many efforts on behalf of the Italian community of Rhode Island, and for his chairing of the committee that published *The Italians and the Creation of America.*Pictured here at the gathering, from left to right, are, Cav. Vincent J. Buonanno Jr.; Vitorio J. Fumo, consul general of Italy in Boston for New England; and Comm. Joseph R. Muratore.

ALEXANDER ADDEO, ENGINEER IN THE FIELD OF STRUCTURAL PROBLEMS. Alexander was an outstanding Italian-American with an enviable professional reputation. Born in Providence, he went on to graduate from Brown University with a BS Degree in Civil Engineering. In 1930, he became Inspector of Construction for the Department of Public Buildings. In 1932, he became Building Inspector of Providence, and many provisions of the Building Code that he helped to formulate are still in effect, not only in Rhode Island, but also throughout the United States. (Courtesy of Gr "Uff" Joseph R. Muratore Collection.)

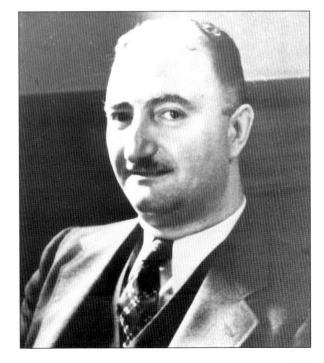

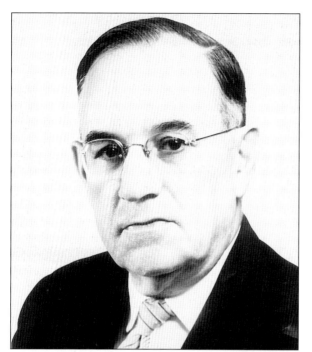

ARCHITECT ORESTO DI SAIA, BORN IN 1900. He graduated Technical High School, and attended several extension courses before establishing his architectural practice 1926. Oresto held every office in the Rhode Island chapter of the American Institute of Architects, including president. He was an active civic leader and was recipient of many service awards. The following are a few of the projects he either designed or supervised the construction of: Uptown Theater; Metropolitan Theatre; Hollywood Theatre; State Hospital for Mental Disease, Howard, RI; the hangar and office building at Theodore Francis Green Airport; Johnston Town Hall; and St. Rocco's Church. (Courtesy of Gr "Uff" Joseph R. Muratore Collection.)

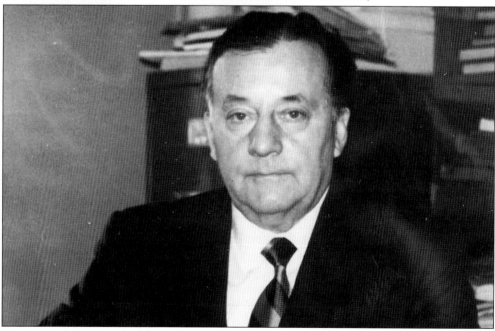

HENRY ISE, ENGINEER. He graduated Brown University, majoring in Hydroelectric and Hydraulic Engineering. With the Water Supply Board, Henry worked as an engineer on the design, development, construction, and operation of the Scituate Water Supply system. He went on to become Chief of Division of Harbors and Rivers, Chairman of the Rhode Island Hurricane Survey Advisory Committee, and President of the Rhode Island Society of Professional Engineers; In 1972, he was named "Engineer of the Year" by the Rhode Island Society of Professional Engineers. (Courtesy of Gr "Uff" Joseph R. Muratore Collection.)

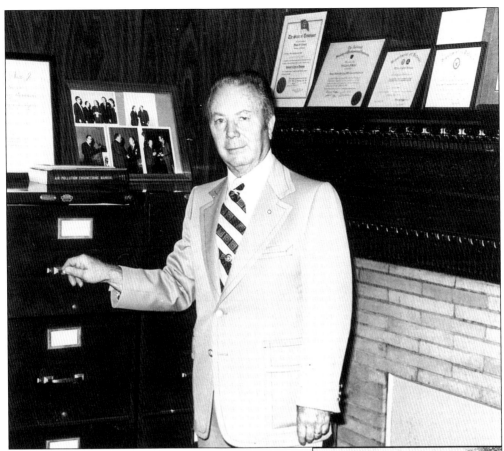

VINCENT DI MASE, DIRECTOR OF THE DEPARTMENT OF BUILDING INSPECTION FOR PROVIDENCE. He graduated from Brown University in 1935. In 1951, he was named Deputy Inspector of Buildings, and, in 1957, Director of the Department of Building Inspection. He has written many magazine articles for Boca, and he was responsible for having 35 cities adopt the Boca Basic Code. He has lectured throughout Rhode Island, and received several awards of merit. The architectural profession has honored his contribution of outstanding service the profession by a "non architect." (Courtesy of Gr "Uff" Joseph R. Muratore Collection.)

ANDREW CARUSO, JUNE 1939. This outstanding mason is shown erecting the statue of Roger William, at Prospect Terrace in Providence. Andrew was recognized as having made a significant contribution in mason artistry throughout Rhode Island. (Courtesy of Gr "Uff" Joseph R. Muratore Collection.)

115

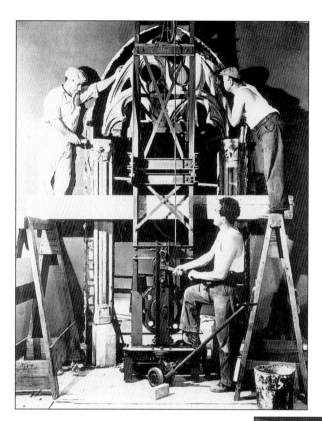

ANDREW CARUSO WITH WORKMEN. They are shown erecting the archway at the Rhode Island School of Design. (Courtesy of Gr "Uff" Joseph R. Muratore Collection.)

HUGO R. MAINELLI JR. In 1938, Hugo formed a partnership and developed the Aetna Bridge Company. Four years later, they formed The Plantations Steel Company, and, later, they founded a completely automated plant in Warwick, Rhode Island. Hugo built more than 100 bridges between Boston and New York, on Interstate 95, Connecticut Turnpike, and the Merritt Parkway. He was truly "A Self Made Man of Steel." (Courtesy of Gr "Uff" Joseph R. Muratore Collection.)

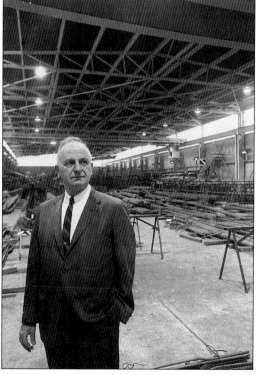

GEORGE DE FELICE, NOTED RHODE ISLAND MURAL ARTIST. George was commissioned to paint a mural representing an image of "Justice," to fill the frame that was originally built to hold the Gilbert Stuart portrait of George Washington, in the Newport county courthouse. He conceived the idea of a painting along the lines of the Roman Classic motif, in soft colors. Although in other portraits of "Justice," she is blindfolded, George painted her without a blindfold; a feature that viewers are quick to comment on. He felt that she should be like a judge sitting in judgment, who would be able to look through you and see that justice prevails. He was one of Rhode Island's most accomplished artists. (Courtesy of Gr "Uff" Joseph R. Muratore Collection.)

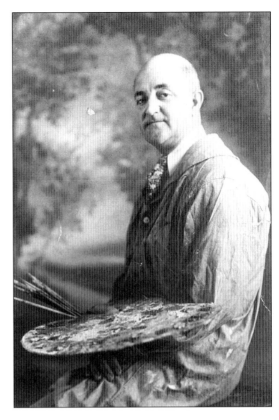

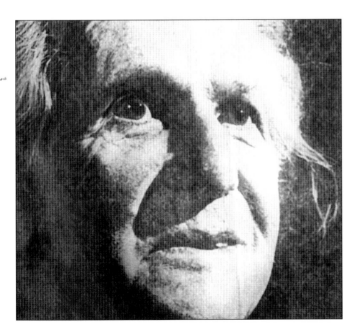

GINO CONTI, ART TEACHER FOR MORE THAN 37 YEARS. This artist followed graduate studies, and received scholarships, from the "Ecole De Beaux Arts" in Fontainebleau, and the Academie Julien in Paris. His works have been on covers of the *Vatican Newspaper*. During the 1930s, he was commissioned to paint murals on the walls of schools and colleges throughout Rhode Island. His technique is reminiscent of Picasso's style. (Courtesy of Gr "Uff" Joseph R. Muratore Collection.)

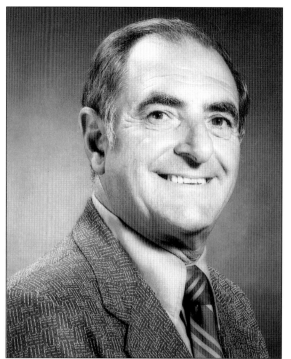

ANGELO MARCELLO, VICE PRESIDENT OF THE C.E. MAGUIRE CONSTRUCTION COMPANY, INC. Angelo graduated from the University of Rhode Island. He is recognized as having extensive experience in heavy civil engineering, for the construction of highways, bridges, dams and public works. The U.S. government decorated him for Meritorious Service. He retired from the U.S. Army as a Lieutenant Colonel. In 1950, he was Director of Public Works for Rhode Island, supervising the construction of miles of expressways and bridges. He was in charge in the initial stages of the Fox Point Hurricane Barrier Dam in Providence. In 1969, he was named "Engineer of the Year" by the Rhode Island Society of Professional Engineers. (Courtesy of Gr "Uff" Joseph R. Muratore Collection.)

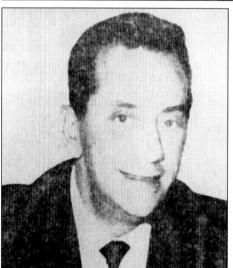

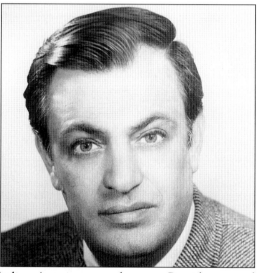

LEFT: LOUIS RUGGIERI, ENGINEER. This Italian-American was born in Providence, and graduated from Old Technical High School before attending the Rhode Island School of Design. He was one of the post-WWII Americans who became a true international engineer. He became head of the engineering firm of Ruggieri & Associates, which had offices in Providence, and Rome in Italy. (Courtesy of Gr "Uff" Joseph R. Muratore Collection.) RIGHT: AMERICO MALLOZZI. He graduated from the Rhode Island School of Design in 1956, and, in 1956-57, he was a Fulbright Scholar at the University of Rome, Italy. He was recipient of several awards, and was a registered architect, nationally and in Rhode Island. In 1974, he established the firm Americo Mallozzi & Associates, in Providence. (Courtesy of Gr "Uff" Joseph R. Muratore Collection.)

JOSEPH A. BERETTA. He is a graduate of the University of Rhode Island, and the Lincoln Institute of Northeastern University. Joseph is former president of the Rhode Island chapter of the American Institute of Architects, as well as the Rhode Island Society of Professional Engineers, and is a former member of the Rhode Island State Board of Registration for Architects. He was president and treasurer of Robinson, Green & Beretta Corporation, one of Rhode Island's largest engineering firms. There are few buildings in Rhode Island that Joseph's firm has not had a part in the design or supervision of. (Courtesy of Gr "Uff" Joseph R. Muratore Collection.)

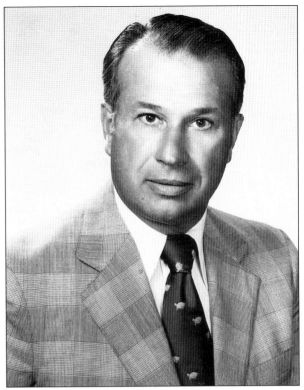

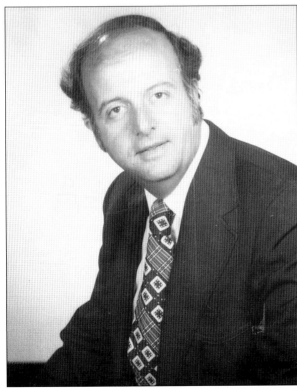

RAYMOND A. DeCESARE, ARCHITECT, AND MEMBER OF ROBINSON, GREEN & BERETTA CORPORATION. Raymond graduated from Rhode Island School of Design in 1970 with a BS degree in Architecture. In 1959, he joined the Robinson Green & Beretta Corporation. He is licensed in Rhode Island, Massachusetts, and Connecticut, and has been a designer and construction supervisor of many buildings throughout the New England area. His many projects include the Knightsville Manor; the Arlington Manor; the Hall Manor, in Cranston; St. Jude's Church, in Lincoln, Rhode Island; St. Augustine's Church, in Melville; and the Centennial Towers in Pawtucket, Rhode Island. (Courtesy of Gr "Uff" Joseph R. Muratore Collection.)

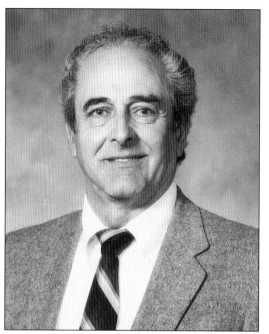

JOSEPH P. MALLOZZI, ARCHITECT. He was born in 1930, in Frosolone, Italy, and then came to America in 1938. He attended Roger Williams University, and the Rhode Island School of Design. A former director of the American Institute of Architects, he is registered in Rhode Island, Connecticut, and Massachusetts. Among the many projects he has designed and supervised, are Fall River Middle School, Campus Master plan, St. John's Preparatory School; St. Joseph's Church and Rectory; Scituate, RI; St. Mark's Church and Rectory; Attleboro Cooperative Bank; Donatelli office building; the ice-skating rink, in Rumford, RI; sports complex, Dartmouth, Mass.; Bonneville Nursing Home; and Medical Center, Woonsocket, RI. Joseph is president of Mallozzi Associates Inc. (Courtesy of Gr "Uff" Joseph R. Muratore Collection.)

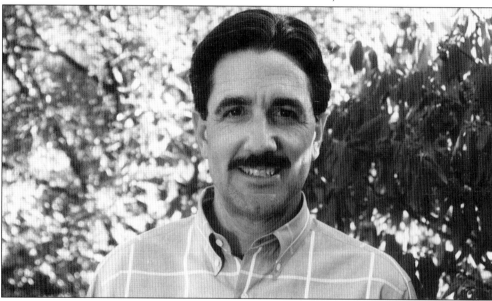

MICHAEL INTEGLIA JR., ARCHITECT. He was born in Providence, and graduated Roger Williams College, in 1969, with a degree of Associate in Architecture. After receiving his BS degree in Construction Engineering in 1970, he attended Harvard University Business School, where he studied Management Accounting, Financing, and Executive Training programs. Michael became president of Michael Integlia & Company; Pavallion Group Real Estate Consortium; Seaview Country Club; and the Summit Condominium Association. He also held the following posts: cost construction manager and pre-construction project manager of Gilbane Building Company, from 1970 to 1974; construction cost estimator for Dimeo Construction, from 1969 to 1970; and interim architect for Oresto Di Saia Associates, from 1968 to 1969. (Courtesy of Gr "Uff" Joseph R. Muratore Collection.)

Seven

RADIO AND TELEVISION, R.I.'S ECHO

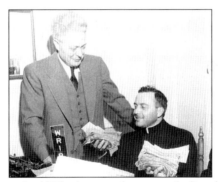

CAVALIERE ANTONIO PACE. In 1935, Antonio began an Italian language program on radio station WPRO. It was through this program, the first of its kind in Rhode Island, that the Italian community was kept informed of activities in Italy and community functions in Rhode Island. During his years of radio service, he took more than 75 trips to Italy, and brought back taped messages from towns that he visited. He played these tapes during his three-hour programs, making it a very popular way for Italian-Americans in Rhode Island to hear familiar voices, even those of loved ones in some cases. His radio programs were later heard on radio stations WRIB and WFCI in Pawtucket. In 1946, with Judge Harold Arcaro and William Considine, Antonio was a cofounder of radio station WRIB. In 1950, the Italian government decorated him, naming him a Cavaliere to the Merit of the Workers of the Republic of Italy. He was born in Percara, Italy, on May 9, 1898, the son of Rocco and Giuseppina (LaBono) Pace. After graduating from the Italian Naval Academy in 1917, he served two years as a lieutenant in the Italian Navy, before immigrating to the United States in 1925. He married Irma DiDomenico, and they were the parents of two children, Harold and Maria (Pace) Candito. After Mrs. Pace died, he married Mary (Fabiano) Pace, and became the stepfather of Robert Fabiano, Mrs. Elizabeth Dockray, and Mrs. Julie Dalpe. Antonio died on August 9, 1977, and is buried in a chapel, which he had constructed, in the Santa Maria del Campo Cemetery, Barrington, R.I. (Courtesy of Gr "Uff" Joseph R. Muratore Collection.)

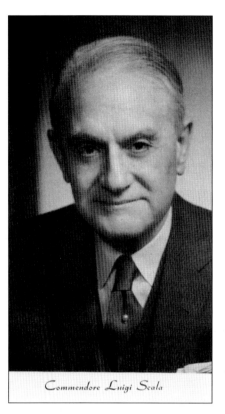

Commendore Luigi Scala

GRANDE UFFICIALE LUIGI SCALA. He was one of the early commentators and announcers of news items on radio, working with Cav. Antonio Pace. Luigi was one of Rhode Island's most illustrious citizens, and was gifted with oratorical splendor, both in Italian and in English. He was born in Sicily, and was an early Royal Italian Consular representative for Louisiana. He came to Providence in 1933, and became president and director of the Columbus National Bank. He was known for his deep understanding of the problems of the early immigrants, and gave guidance and assistance freely. He retired as president of Columbus National in 1967. Luigi was born in Miliazzo, Sicily, Italy, the son of Felice and Maria Scala. He married Marjorie (McGuire) Scala, and they had no children. It was his wish to be buried next to his mother in Milazzo, Sicily. He died on August 28, 1975, and the author made the necessary arrangements for his wish to be carried out. (Courtesy of Gr "Uff" Joseph R. Muratore Collection.)

CAVALIERE VINCENZO LENTINI, FOUNDER OF THE ITALIAN WAR VETERANS OF WORLD WAR I. He was instrumental in having Italian Veterans to obtain their war decorations from Italy. Prior to the author becoming the Italian Vice Consul for Rhode Island, Cav. Lentini was the Italian Consular correspondent for Rhode Island. He was a very dedicated and tireless worker for whatever project he undertook. He was active in many Italian-American patriotic endeavors, and was an outstanding orator in Italian. He was decorated, in 1966, by the Italian government, who named him Cavaliere, in the Order to the Merit of the Republic of Italy. Vincenzo was born in Casamassima Bare, Italy, on October 13, 1896, the son of Francesco Lentini and Maria Paolai (Barone) Lentini. He graduated from the Victor Emanuele Technical Institute in Melfi Potenza, Italy. On November 8, 1923, he married Antoneete (Mariorano) Lentini, in Providence, and they were the parents of three children, Mary Estelle Salvatore, Grace Dolores Curtellessa, and Robert Joseph. (Courtesy of Gr "Uff" Joseph R. Muratore Collection.)

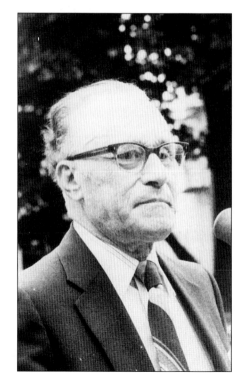

CLAUDE CAMPELLONE. He produced and broadcast a weekly Italian radio program from WKRI for many years. After immigrating from Colli al Volturno Compobasso, Italy, in 1929, he settled in Providence.He was a graduate of Providence College, receiving a degree in literature in 1936, after which, he attended Brown University, where he studied law for two years. For many years, he taught Italian in Cranston High Schools. He served in the U.S. Air Force as a lieutenant in Algiers, Italy, France, Germany, and Austria. After WWII, he studied French Literature in Sobonne, Paris, where he met his future wife, Jeanne M. (Gerraud) Campellone. They were married at the Notre Dame Cathedral in 1949, and they became the parents of two children, Mary Anne and John C. For a time, he was publisher of *The Echo* of Rhode Island. In 1954, when Antonio Pace retired, Claude bought the Italian radio program from him. (Courtesy of Gr "Uff" Joseph R. Muratore Collection.)

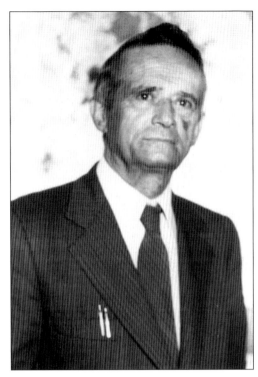

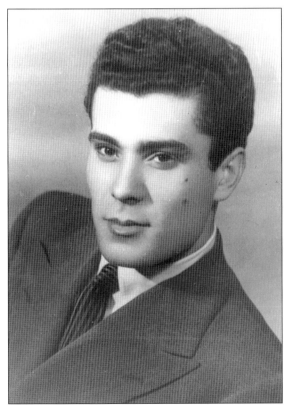

CAVALEIRE ROLANDO PETRELLA, BROADCASTING DIRECTOR OF THE VOICE OF ITALY FOR 40 YEARS. The *Voice of Italy* was a pioneer program that served as a link to Italy. Rolando was born in Caserta, Italy, where he attended Salvatore Pozzi College and served in the Italian Special Police Force, before coming to Rhode Island in 1951. He was active in many civic, religious, and fraternal organizations, and his program was a regular feature of radio station WRIB. Rolando raised large sums of monies for flood and earthquake victims of Italy. In 1992, he was presented the Star of Solidarity, in the rank of Cavaliere, in the Order to the Merit of the Republic of Italy. The high standards that he established for his programs, and the excellent music he presented, made his program very popular with Italian-Americans in Rhode Island. After his death, Maria Gina Aiello continued his radio program. (Courtesy of Gr "Uff" Joseph R. Muratore Collection.)

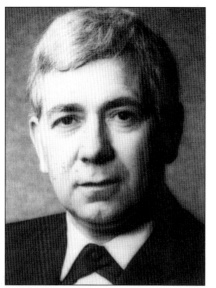

CAVALIERE VIRGILIO DEVECCHIS. Born in Italy in 1924, he attended the University of Rhode Island for two years, then took a three-year home study course with the Central Technical Institute, Hartford, Connecticut. He also took extension courses in broadcasting, and is fluent in three languages, Italian, French and English. Prior to his retirement, Virgilio was employed by the Hemphill Company, Taco Heathers, Gorham Manufacturing, and Brown & Sharp. He was commentator and announcer on several Rhode Island Italian-American radio programs, broadcasting for station WYNG of Warwick, WKFD of Wakefield, and WRIB of Providence. He is currently a volunteer lobbyist for the American Association of Retired Persons. In 1949, he married Mary (Coccio) DeVecchis in Rome, Italy, and they were the parents of two children, Rose Bugli (deceased) and David. (Gr "Uff" Joseph R. Muratore Collection.)

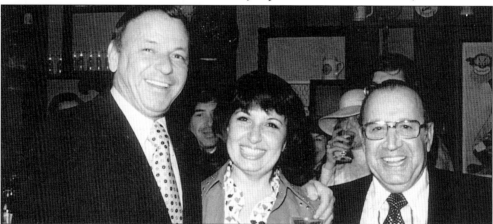

FRANK SINATRA, CARMEL MARLIN (MANCINI) MALIGNAGGI, AND JOSEPH P. MALIGNAGGI. Joseph was born in 1921 in Providence. After attending Providence schools, he left Rhode Island in 1940, and graduated from the Julliard School of Music. He organized the orchestra that provided the music for Frank Sinatra's personal tours, television appearances, and recordings. Joseph became Sinatra's concertmaster and booking agent for New England, and worked for him from 1964 until his death in 1994. He recorded with practically every well-known star of the time, including Barbara Streisand, Perry Como, Tony Bennett, Elvis Presley, John Lennon, Paul McCartney, Steven Lawrence, and Edie Gorme. He also worked on many films for Henry Mancini, organizing Mancini's band. He met his wife, Carmel Marlin* (Mancini), while they were students at the Julliard School of Music. They married in 1949, and were the parents of Mary and Paul Malignaggi. Mary Marlin is a Hollywood Emmy-winning costume designer, and Paul is a production manager, producing performances and works with Liza Mannelli, Michael Feinstein, and Frank Sinatra Jr. Joseph died on November 6, 1994. His wife has continued as a musician with the Sinatra group and is their booking agent for New England and New York. Joseph was the son of Maria (Ferla) and Paul Maglignaggi, a violin maker and barber. His mother is 100 years old, lives in Rhode Island, and is the sister of Conrad Ferla.*Marlin is the professional name assumed by the Malignaggi family. (Courtesy of Gr "Uff" Joseph R. Muratore Collection.)

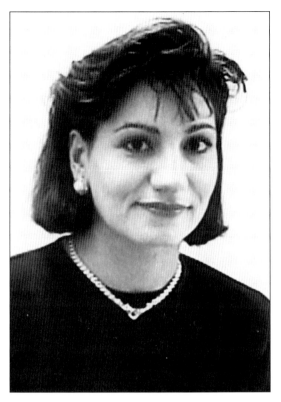

MARIA GINA AIELLO. Maria was born in the province of Catanzaro, Calabria, Italy, the daughter of Saverio and Teresa (Mazza) Aiello. She attended public school in Scuole Medie, Italy, before coming to America with her family in 1970, and took courses in journalism at University of Rhode Island. In 1970, she began her radio career as an announcer on the *Voice of Italy* program on station WRIB, Providence. She produced and hosted the first bilingual program in Rhode Island, and became assistant director. In 1998, when Cav. Rolando Petrella died, she became director and host of the *Voice of Italy*. Maria has one daughter, Azzurra G. Catucci, who was born in 1994. (Courtesy of Gr "Uff" Joseph R. Muratore Collection.)

FRANKIE N. CARLE, "WIZARD" OF THE KEYBOARD. He was born Francis Nunzio Carlone, on March 25, 1903, in Providence. As well as being was one of the most popular pianists of the 1940s and '50s, he composed "Sunrise Serenade," which became the theme song of Glenn Miller. Starting in 1916, Frankie worked with the biggest-name bands in America. He was a featured performer, and later, a partner in the Horace Heidt Orchestra, which he left, in 1944, to form his own band. His daughter, billed as Marjorie Hughs, was the featured singer of this band. Carle had several million-copy sellers in the late 40s and early 50s. In 1955, he disbanded the orchestra, and thereafter, he performed mainly as a soloist. Some of his recordings include Frankie Carle's "Dance Parade," "Sunrise Serenade," "Mediterranean Cruise," "30 Hits Of The Thundering 30s," and "30 Hits of the Flaming 30s." His orchestra was a great favorite in America's top clubs, ballrooms and theaters. He now makes his home with his daughter in Nevada. (Courtesy of Gr "Uff" Joseph R. Muratore Collection.)

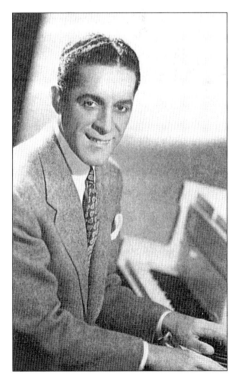

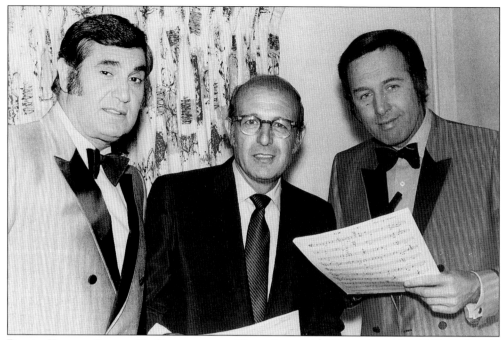

RALPH YOUNG, JOSEPH V. CRIBARI, AND TONY SANDLER. Throughout the 1960s and early 70s, Joseph was musical director and conductor for the singing team of Sandler and Young. (Courtesy of Gr "Uff" Joseph R. Muratore Collection.)

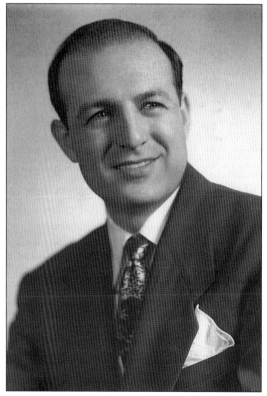

JOSEPH V. (JOE) CRIBARI, PIANIST EXTRAORDINAIRE, ARRANGER, AND CONDUCTOR. Joseph became Glenn Miller's arranger, and produced the unusual musical arrangements for the world-famous Glenn Miller Band. He was born on July 15, 1920, in Providence, the son of Phyllis (Ferrante) Cribari and Joseph F. Cribari, although they later became residents of Warwick, RI. He began piano lessons at five years old, and went on to graduate from LaSalle Academy. In 1939, he left Rhode Island and went to Rye Beach, New York, where he joined the Tommy Reynold's Band and then began to play with Sammy Kaye, Victor Lombardo, Ray McKinley, Glenn Miller, and Tommy Dorsey. He became affiliated with the Glenn Miller Band, and, as an arranger and musical coordinator, he created the haunting Miller style of sound. He married Jane (Griffin) Cribari in 1953, and they were the parents of two children, Linda and Joseph. (Courtesy of Gr "Uff" Joseph R. Muratore Collection.)

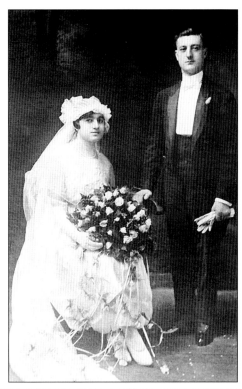

Joseph V. Cribari's Parents, on Their Wedding Day, September 10, 1919. Filomena Phyllis (Ferrante) and Joseph F. Cribari were the parents of four children, Joseph, Doris, Robert, and Donald. (Courtesy of Gr "Uff" Joseph R. Muratore Collection.)

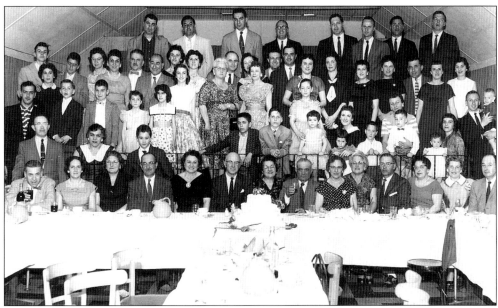

Ferrante Family Reunion Dinner. This occasion was held at the 1025 Club, Providence, in September of 1958. Some of the family members at the head table, pictured here from left to right, are Frank Manzo, Rose (Ferrante) Manzo; Vera (Ferrante) Olobri, Lucio Ferrante, Emma (Ferrante) Caliri; Pasquale Ferrante, Phyllis (Ferrante) Cribari, Michael Mainelli, Etta (Ferrante) Gliottone, Nicholas Leone, Celia (Bonafiglia) Leone, Madeline (Lanfredi) Ferrante, and Albert Ferrante. (Courtesy of Gr "Uff" Joseph R. Muratore Collection.)

127

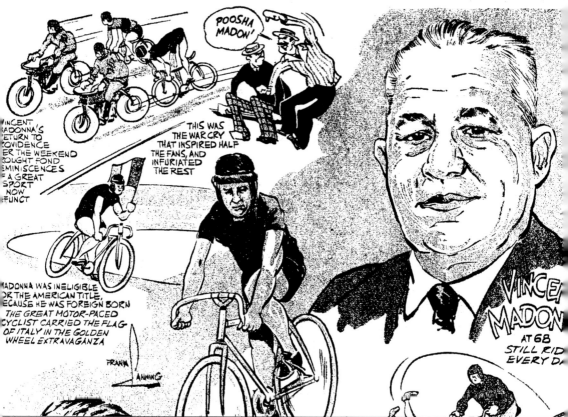

VINCENT MADONNA, "UNCROWNED BICYCLE CHAMPION." He was a well-known figure in Rhode Island. Although an outstanding cyclist, he was ineligible for the American Cyclist Title because he was foreign born. Vincent carried the Italian Flag in the Golden Wheel Extravaganza. He was cheered and encouraged by fans, who would shout "Poosha Madonna," meaning "Push-God." This was the haunting cheer that inspired the fans who gave resounding support to Vincent Madonna during cycle races. (Courtesy of Gr "Uff" Joseph R. Muratore Collection.)